Let Us Sing

*Improve Your Skills,
Improve Your Choir*

A Brief Guide for the
New or Untrained Choir Director

Wayne Moore

Lutheran University Press
Minneapolis, Minnesota

Let Us Sing

Improve Your Skills, Improve Your Choir
A Brief Guide for the New or Untrained Choir Director
by Wayne Moore

Copyright 2013 Lutheran University Press, an imprint of 1517 Media. All rights reserved. No part of this publication may be reproduced, stored in a retrieval system, or transmitted in any form or by any means, electronic, mechanical, photocopying, recording, or otherwise, without written permission of the publisher: 1517 Media Permissions, PO Box 1209, Minneapolis, MN 55440-1209, or copyright@1517.media.

Library of Congress Cataloging-in-Publication Data

Moore, Wayne, 1964-
  Let us sing : improve your skills, improve your choir : a brief guide for the new or untrained choir director / Wayne Moore.
     p. cm.
  Includes bibliographical references.
  ISBN 978-1-932688-77-1 (alk. paper) – ISBN 1-932688-77-3 (alk. paper) – eISBN 978-1-942304-64-7
  1. Choirs (Music) 2. Singing. I. Title.
  MT88.M79 2012
  782.5'145—dc23
                    2012034593

Contents

Introduction 5

PART ONE: THE ABCs OF CHOIR DIRECTING

The Choral Experience 11

    Auditions 14

    Repertoire 15

    Warm-ups 17

    Rehearsals 17

    Balancing the Voice Parts 20

    Conducting Basics 22

    The Trainer in You 24

    Accompaniment 26

    The "P" Person 27

PART TWO: PRACTICALS

Preparing the Score Notes 31

    Carol: "Ding dong! merrily on high" arr. Charles Wood

    Motet: *Lord For Thy Tender Mercy's Sake* by Richard Farrant

    Anthem: *Jesu, joy of man's desiring* by J. S. Bach

    Folk gospel: "Count Your Blessings" arr. Edwin Excell

    Major anthem: "Hallelujah Chorus" by G. F. Handel

Management and the Next Generation 61

PART THREE: VOCALIZATION

Basic Vocal Anatomy 67
    Breath Management .... .75
    Phonation, Resonation, Registration................................... .79
    Intonation Control and Enunciation .... .84
Taking Care of Your Voice 92
    Vocal Warm-Up Exercises.. 93
Summary .... .100
Glossary of Terms... 101
About the Author 104

Introduction

I have seen many choir directors struggle with the job of teaching and performing music to an acceptable standard. Directing the average church choir is particularly difficult, because the members are often untrained. Traditional church choirs are frequently comprised of older persons whose voices are at the twilight of their useful vocal years. This poses a special challenge when it comes to breath control and tone. Additionally, in most contemporary, charismatic churches, the number of female voices overwhelms the male voices, leaving no chance to sing soprano, alto, tenor, bass (SATB) music.

The average church choir director's world can, at times, be lonely and frustrating. Every rehearsal seems like *deja vu*. The tenors forgot what they were taught last time, and the altos still can't quite get it. Because some of the female sopranos are "belters," every piece of choral music is pitched too high for them, and you have to limit your repertoire to contemporary choruses. Everyone has a favorite piece of music that's perfect for the choir, and advisers are falling over each other to tell you what you should be performing. At times the choice is between a "one man band" and "management by committee." Either way, criticisms come readily, and encouragement is only to be found in one's own inner drive and spiritual commitment.

Youth choir directors have a special challenge. First, there is the competition between the singing styles of traditional choral music and popular contemporary songs. Second, there is the competition between the choir and every other activity in the rest of their life. Third, adolescent minds are often hard to focus. The kids tend to be difficult to settle into a disciplined routine, and they have no patience to learn challenging or, in the view of the adolescent mind, "boring" choral repertoire. Fourth, the resources to do the job are often lacking. The biggest question is "How do we draw the interests and energy of youth toward the choral art form, when all around them, in every form of media, there are popular forms of music which seem much more fun and accessible?" Which teenager walks around with an iPod listening to Handel or Mozart? And worse, what "normal" teenager dares to play Bach in front of his peers? This is the "belter's world;" rock, rap, reggae, calypso, R & B, gospel, pop, and whatever else is on the popular menu, are the mainstream musical styles which captivate the youngsters. Today's kids are fed a steady diet of belting tones from church to school, iPod to cable to internet. Yes, traditional choral vocal styles are a strange concept to them, for this is a new era of music. Nevertheless, it is possible to find the few who will take on classical training and thankfully there are some excellent school choirs out there, but the choir director will need know-how to keep the youngsters interested and enthusiastic.

I have tried to make the material in this book as concise as possible while still presenting essential details. It is not possible to cover the full scope of the material necessary for a comprehensive academic and instructional manual within this book. Indeed, there are many colleges which offer in-depth choral training courses. Nothing here is guaranteed, because results will vary according to your effort and circumstances. Some of the exercises described in this book may be physically challenging. Persons are advised to seek medical advice before undertaking these exercises.

It is my hope that through this modest handbook you will be able to improve both yourself and your choir, and increase the personal satisfaction you get from teaching and performing choral music. If you are a high school teacher who has been asked to take the choir and you don't have a clue but you want to succeed, this is your start. If you are a church choir member and you have been asked to take over when the current director retires, this is your start. If you are an aspiring singer and you want to learn how to do a better job of singing, this is your start. Note that I say "start," because every day we all learn something more, and nothing beats formal training in the appropriate setting.

Most important of all is that you, the choir director, must first learn and practice before you can teach. For this purpose, I have intentionally included vocal instruction which will allow you, the director, to engage in your own vocal development and lead by example.

I must give recognition to my wife, Andrea, who encouraged me to put this book together.

Part One

The ABCs of Choir Directing

The Choral Experience

*"Synergy—the bonus that is achieved
when things work together harmoniously."*
Mark Twain

A choir is defined as an organized group of singers, usually more than twelve, often singing in the context of a church, but not exclusively. Interestingly, a choir is also the term used for a particular order of angels and certain sections of an orchestra. Choral singing is an art which has its roots in European culture; the earliest confirmed record of choral music is that of second century Greece. The earliest notated music began with the simple Gregorian chant. Choral music has evolved through many stages or periods (Medieval, Renaissance, Baroque, Classical, Romantic, Neo-Classical, Modern, etc.), each characterized by an explosion of exceptional composers (Palestrina, Lassus, Morley, Byrd, Handel, Mozart, Wesley, Bainton, Bernstein, Britten, to present day Rutter, Hogan, etc.). Each of these composers furthered the development of choral music, not only by writing musical notation, but also by applying their exceptional understanding of the abilities of the human voice, thus, bringing out its beauty and drama in song. Early choirs were modest in size, usually consisting of between ten and fourteen singers. Today it is not uncommon to find choirs with upwards of 200 singers. However, the size of the choir does not determine its quality. Choral music is not confined to any particular culture, but, rather, it transcends all cultures and is adapted to fit into the nuances which characterize each culture.

Modern choral music is very demanding on the vocal abilities of singers. It requires artful as well as technical employment of pitch and rhythm nuances. The more recent use of sophisticated electronic instruments to enhance choral presentations has been a mixed bag in terms of the effect on the art. On one hand, there is no doubt that the electronic instruments have assisted the dynamic aspects of choral music, but on the other hand some forms of choral music rely too heavily on instrumental augmentations and too little on the art of singing, which of course is the essence of choral music.

Good choral singing requires talent, teamwork, patience, and considerable practice. Choir directors have to understand the nature of musical language and the technical aspects of the human voice. Individual singers must also appreciate both the possibilities and limitations of their own voices, and how they fit into the matrix of other voices to make music.

Choral singing imposes a number of responsibilities on the singer. First of all, the singer must have proper technique to create a pleasing tone with sufficient range and power to deliver the music easily. Second, the singer must be able to sing accurate pitch relative to the other singers. Third, the singer must also have the aptitude to interpret the meaning of the text and to convert that understanding to vocal production. The singer must understand beauty, sorrow, joy, anger, reverence, excitement, when and how to crescendo or place emphasis, and how to use tone to sing out without standing out. The singer must be able to accurately reproduce the text in the dialect of the language in which the music is written, especially the production and pronunciation of vowels. A good singer must be able to read notation fluently.

Young children, in particular, can benefit from the choral experience because the intellectual challenges and discipline of corporate music-making have been shown to stimulate the general learning process and develop a sense of focus, diligence, aesthetic appreciation, and teamwork. Music-making engages both hemispheres of the brain and helps in the early development of synaptic connections and neuron paths, and is carried over into other areas of development. Studies conducted by the University of Toronto, Mississuaga, in 2004, have produced a report, "Music Lessons Enhance IQ," which found that the so-called "Mozart effect" might be more than just a chance observation. The study was conducted on a number of children below the age of seven years. There were four groups of children: one group had keyboard lessons, a second group had singing lessons, a third group had drama lessons, and the fourth group had no lessons at all. The result of the tests showed the greatest improvement in IQ test scores among the choral music group, followed by the group that had keyboard lessons, and then the group that had drama lessons. The test group had a slight improvement as well, possibly due to the test environment. Music lessons have real benefits which apparently touch other non-musical areas of development. Learning vocal music requires extended periods of focused attention, frequent practice, learning and reading notation, memorizing passages, progressive mastery of technical skills, as well as emotional and expressive behavior. Singing requires the integration and coordination of the body and intellect.

The choral experience is a team experience. Although members may not be excellent singers individually, the group effort magnifies the individuals and provides an environment where the intellectual and artistic abilities of each person can find a valid place. From the church choir director's perspective, the choir is much more than music. It is a vehicle for praise and worship of God. Indeed, it is spiritually fulfilling to perform a piece of music after weeks of hard rehearsals, to see it received enthusiastically by the assembly, and to know that everything was done correctly.

The Holy Bible underlines the relevance, power, and effectiveness of a choir when King Jehoshaphat's army was led into battle by a choir of men in 2 Chronicles 20:21: "After consulting the people, Jehoshaphat appointed men to sing to the Lord and to praise him for the splendor of his holiness as they went out at the head of the army, saying: 'Give thanks to the Lord, for his love endures forever.'" The greatest pieces of choral music are not written by mere commission of man, but rather, have been placed into the souls of great composers at a time when they were contemplating the beauty and glory of God. The results have been a rich legacy from which we can all draw inspiration as we contemplate God's majesty.

AUDITIONS

"The prime function of a leader is to keep hope alive."
John W. Gardner

The choir director's first job is to select and sort the voices. This is done in an audition. In order to hold a successful audition, the director must have a good idea of what to look for. The director must have a clear understanding of the type of choir and the technical level of music which will be performed.

The average church or school choir director has to work with the people who volunteer to sing in the choir. Thus, the audition process is largely short-circuited. Sometimes however, an "audition" process can help re-sort the voices, which will be helpful as the director assembles the choir and chooses the repetoire.

First, you need to know several things about the singer who attends the audition:

Age. In the case of a children's choir, the treble should ideally be between nine and ten years old to start, although older children can also make the grade. Generally, you do not want a very wide variation in the ages of singers in a treble line because this can present tone matching issues. There is also a danger in using young voices to fill adult voice parts.

Singing experience. What is the singer's background and exposure? Is the singer accustomed to a particular style of singing which might require significant effort to fit into the culture of your choir? A singer who has practiced the *bel canto* style of singing could have a problem with some modern gospel music. Similarly, if your group is not very literate in terms of musical notation, a person who is fluent in sight reading might very soon become frustrated. Neither is necessarily a reason to reject a singer, but it does give the director insights as the rehearsal process begins.

Motive. Why does the singer want to be a part of the group? Choral music-making requires significant commitment. A singer must therefore want to be in the choir for the right reasons.

Next, you need to hear the voice and get an idea of the singer's abilities by paying attention to the following qualities:

Tone should be clear and resonant, but must also reasonably match the current singers or an established ideal singer.

Range should be at least an octave and a half.

Volume should be capable of singing *piano* (soft) to *forte* (loud).

Pitch should be able to sing with semi-tone accuracy and reproduce a simple melody accurately after listening to it twice.

I usually have a rating scale of one to five for each of these areas.

And finally, if you are privileged to have a large number of people audition, you can pick the best of the best for your choir. There are, of course, other important things to look for in a singer, such as poise, personality, and, if possible, the singer's intelligence level. Young people especially tend to grasp musical concepts and perform better if they have a good academic aptitude. Have a conversation with each singer and try to understand their motivations and their abilities.

REPERTOIRE

What should the choir sing? This is a difficult issue. Every choir director has a preference in terms of the type of music which he likes personally. This can at times conflict with the music which the choir is able to successfully learn and perform. For example, teaching Bernstein's "Chichester Psalms" to six year olds is absurd. On the other hand, we don't want to be teaching "Five Little Speckled Frogs" to our church choir for presentation at worship. The repertoire is very important to the success of the choir. High school singers usually gravitate toward popular contemporary music, like rap and pop. However, such music is not "choral" as presented by the pop singers. It is possible to compose choral arrangements of these songs, but this takes time, so be prepared for the challenge.

Also, teaching kids to discover and use their singing voice in a healthy way means not encouraging the habit of overly using the chest voice to the detriment of the head voice, as tends to occur with most popular music. This is a very important point. Modal voice, or the singer's natural speaking voice, is quite acceptable and is by far the most popular form of vocal expression. However, as the young voice develops, the child will lose the ability to understand the use of their head tones if their repertoire is based on chest register level music only. Notice, also for this reason, that many gospel choirs do not really have the conventional soprano, alto, tenor, and bass vocal categories. Instead, there are high, middle, and low voices, all within the modal-level voice range. These choirs tend to have difficulty singing traditional choral music, even hymns, because the modal voice cannot comfortably handle the higher vocal range required for the performance of this type of music.

Sometimes the music is transposed down in order to avoid high notes, but this is limiting. Therefore, I suggest choir directors develop a mix of traditional choral music as well as some contemporary styles in their repertoire. In particular, school choir directors must ensure that traditional choral music forms the core of their repertoire. This will allow the students to develop proper vocal technique. Choral music need not be traditional, and it need not be ancient. But it needs to be sufficiently challenging and relevant to exercise the choir's ability and give them practice in reading music and utilizing the vocal techniques which are taught later in this book. I find that spirituals can be appealing to high school kids and still accomplish the vocal development objectives. My personal preference is for any choral music which will showcase the beauty of the human voice, so I lean toward unaccompanied music.

You must remember that the reason for vocal classifications is that individuals have different vocal ranges and timbres. If a person cannot sing a good soprano F5 above middle C then they are not likely to be a soprano, Perhaps alto would be best. Similarly, a bass who cannot sing a good low G2 is no bass. The choir director has to place the voices where they fit best.

WARM-UPS

Why is it necessary to warm up? Well let us take a very brief look at what is involved in the muscular action of the larynx.

The vocal folds are delicate muscular tissues. They have a fine web of blood vessels running their length and depend on a proper blood supply to function efficiently. As the vocal muscles stretch and relax, we do not want to put undue stress on the muscles before the blood circulation reaches the correct level. Just as athletes must warm up their muscles before vigorous training or competition, singers must also warm up their vocal muscles. It is necessary to start the muscular action, wake up the blood supply, and then increase the muscular action which stimulates the blood supply even more, until the full level of circulation is achieved.

If a proper warm-up is not done, you can be certain that the delicate vocal apparatus will suffer some level of damage. This could accumulate over time and result in trauma to the vocal folds. Anyone aspiring to be a good singer (whether classical, gospel, or pop), will find that their aspirations will be short-lived if they sing demanding music without a proper warm-up routine.

An appropriate warm-up routine will activate the body, breathing, and voice.

Body:
- Stretch upward.
- With hands over head, stretch to the left then to the right.
- Torso twist left and right, arms at shoulder-level, elbows bent.
- Turn head and neck slowly to the left, hold; then to the right.

Breathing:
- Stand with bouyant posture.
- Raise arms, inhale fully and hold; exhale, "tsss," hold; release.
- Inhale and hum a note; hold the tone for a slow count of eight; repeat and increase to ten and so on, up to a count of twenty.

- Hold a square piece of tissue paper in front of your mouth and gently blow.
- Keep the breath pressure up so that the paper stays away from you until your air runs out; repeat.

Vocalizing:
- Hum a pentatonic scale (imagine bees in a jar).
- Do lip trills.
- Sing, "goo, goo, goo" or "lee, lee, lee" starting from a mid-chest voice pitch (G3), and work up to C5 above middle C, ascending and descending.

Choral voice exercises should generally be done in a group setting. Since it is useful for the voices to have a smooth grading and uniform tone from the low voices to the high voices, a degree of tone matching is necessary. Tone matching simply ensures that when the group sings in unison the tone is clean and uniform. In addition, there are times when a piece of music will require two adjacent voice parts, for example tenor and alto, to sing the same pattern of notes, imitating each other. Additionally, within each voice part, soprano, alto, tenor, or bass, tone matching is essential. Each singer must develop the keenness to adjust to the other person's tone.

At times, voice parts may need to be separated. For example, vocalizers which are designed to build particular tones should be confined to the voice parts for which the exercises are designed.

Vocalizing exercises using the "oo" and "ee" vowel sound help to build head tone. Ensure that the singers place their tongue low in the mouth. The exercises should be done in a descending pitch, in order to strengthen the head tone resonance at the lower pitch (like a wolf howl). Trebles, sopranos, altos, and tenors would benefit from this exercise. Vocalizing exercises using the "ah" vowel sound help "open" the tone and strengthen resonance at all pitch levels. However, the tongue must be low at the back of the throat, and the jaw and lips should be relaxed. There are more vocal warm-up exercises for building choral tone included at the end of this book.

REHEARSALS

The greatest challenge of the choir director is to maintain the enthusiasm and momentum of the group, year in and year out. One way to do this is to increase the musical challenges each year. Find interesting arrangements of familiar music or attempt a difficult or unusual piece of music. Another way is to let your group do recordings. This can be very effective, because each recording represents a new frontier which drives the group's interest. In addition, recording frequently sharpens the group's technical and aesthetic abilities; you would be amazed at the effect you get when you hear yourself in a recording. Visiting other churches as a guest choir is also a good way of keeping the group's interest.

Most church choirs rehearse after work. Although this is possibly the worst time to have a rehearsal, it is often the only time available. Usually, there is time for only one rehearsal per week. The choir director has the challenging task of making amateur singers perform like as a focused, unified choir within this limited time. Therefore, let us look at a few ideas to make the rehearsal as productive as possible.

First of all, plan the rehearsal carefully. Study the music and determine how you will proceed. Allocate time for each element of the rehearsal. Second, everyone needs to be on time! The choir director should always be first to arrive and last to leave. Then, the rehearsal must start on time regardless of whether everyone is present or not. Make it a point to speak to any latecomers at the end of the rehearsal, urging them to promptness.

Ensure that the rehearsal facility is well lit and ventilated. The singers need to have adequate drinking water (room temperature). Avoid air conditioning as much as possible. Most churches have a dedicated place for choir rehearsals, but if not, the facility needs to be prepared ahead of the arrival of the choir in order to minimize the disruptive assembly of chairs.

Develop a routine for your rehearsals. This will encourage discipline and help the singers settle down quickly. Allocate specific time slots for warm-ups, vocal exercises, and post-rehearsal discussions. Begin with a few minutes of loosening up and relaxation, and plan for at least ten minutes of ear exercises and breath control exercises at the beginning of each rehearsal.

Comfortable seating is important, but have the singers stand when they are actually singing a learned section. This will build stamina and reinforce good posture and breathing habits. If it becomes necessary for the singers to sit while singing, they should sit upright and forward on the seat, with shoulders slightly back.

Keep the atmosphere lively and brisk. If boredom sets in, change the position of the singers, discuss a light topic, or change the music. Encourage laughter, which releases endorphins, adding to the pleasantry of the rehearsal. Do not tolerate chatter—one of the best ways to waste a lot of time and frustrate others. Always begin a new piece of music by explaining the background of the music, your expectations, the composer's expectations, and, possibly, the listener's expectations. It sets the tone in the singers' minds and, importantly, puts them on the same plane with you, the director.

Work first with the line which will grasp the music quickest. Then add the others gradually. Depending on the competence level of the group, you could tackle blocks of music at a time. Be sure that each block is properly understood. During the learning process, let the singers know what you require in terms of dynamics, tone quality, breathing, diction, etc. Reinforce these ideas with conducting gestures. The intention is to let the choir rehearse not only the music, but also the performance of it. Some groups have instrumental accompaniment. Whether this is a band, a solo instrument, or an orchestra, they should rehearse separately from the choir. At the point where the choir has really grasped the music, the two groups can come together. It is not feasible to rehearse both groups in detail simultaneously without wasting one group's time. There will be a period of re-learning as the two groups "iron out their differences." A skillful director will guide the process, and the final result will not betray the difficulties encountered along the way.

BALANCING THE VOICE PARTS

When we look at a choral ensemble performing, we are immediately drawn to the fact that the singers are arranged in some kind of order. This order is usually based on the voice parts, but sometimes there is no apparent logic to the order, and the group is merely a jumble of singers.

There should always be an order to the assembly of performing singers. Singers should have adequate room around them in the ensemble; that is, about an elbow's length on either side and about an arm's length in front and behind. This will improve the choir's sound presence as well as allow each singer to hear the ensemble.

We will now look at a few patterns and the rationale behind them. Remember, we are dealing with amateur groups in the typical church or high school choir.

When the choir is made up of predominantly female voices, the director has a challenge in allowing the males to be heard (and seen). The convention is to place the males in the rear and the females in front; sometimes there are several rows of females in front of the males. The solution to this situation is to place the males in a block of two or three rows at the side of the females (figure A). From the aesthetic standpoint, this could look clumsy, but the auditory trade-off is worth it.

BBBSSSSSAAA
TTTSSSSSAAA
Conductor

FIGURE A

Another problem occurs when the males are not only small in number but lack the confidence to stand on their own. Males in this type of group will need to be placed in the middle of the front and possibly also the second row as well. The director will then be able to give them direct attention and guidance (figure B).

AASSBBBSSAA
SSSSTTTSSSS
Conductor

FIGURE B

A good rule of thumb is that you need to have as many sopranos as altos, tenors, and basses combined. This depends on the relative strengths of the voice parts. Generally, if there are four of each of the lower parts (alto, tenor, bass), then there should be twelve sopranos. When the ratio is biased to more sopranos, the tone will be bright and transparent, the words will be clear, but there will be a lack of "fullness" and the harmony will lack balance. Too few sopranos, and the tone will be very meaty and rich, and somewhat lacking in clarity and definition. However, as I said before, one has to also bear in mind the quality of the voices and not just the numbers. If the sopranos are good, then you will not need as many. As director, you will have to assess the actual sound balance and decide on the practical numbers. One always has to work with what is available. Bear in mind that in a church choir, it is always easier to add than to subtract.

Whenever possible the strongest voices should be placed close to the center of the group. The arrangement which I find to work best (with an ideal balance of voices), is one where the ATB are arranged in one line at the back and the sopranos are arranged in the front line, with the strongest sopranos in the middle. The altos and tenors are split into two groups flanking the basses. In this way the choir is able to fill the sound stage and can also hear each other properly (figure C).

A A T T B B B B T T A A
S S S S S S S S S S
Conductor
FIGURE C

A possible alternative to the arrangement in figure C is a variation where the ATB are not split but are grouped in blocks. If your ATB are not competent enough to be split, then this will be a good arrangement as well (figure D).

A A A A B B B B T T T T
S S S S S S S S S S S S
Conductor
FIGURE D

Some conductors use an arrangement in which there is a mixing of the voice parts throughout the ensemble. The objective here is to expand the sound field of the choir. To some extent, this technique works. The drawback to this arrangement is that the conductor cannot really cue a particular voice part for entry, cut-off, or dynamic embellishment, and this can lead to confusion. This is not for the novice. The choir members have to really know the music (figure E).

S A B S T S B S S T A S

T S A B S T S S S A B S

Conductor

FIGURE E

CONDUCTING BASICS

The choir director must guide and control the music as it is being presented. The director is, in fact, playing one of the grandest of instruments. There are as many styles of conducting as there are conductors. However, basic rules still underlie the individual's stylistic platform.

The objectives of conducting are:

1. To provide a visual cue for the start and end of the music.
2. To provide visual cues for the tempo.
3. To give interpretive guidance to the singers.
4. To coordinate the voice parts and musical accompaniment.

The general rules of good conducting are:

1. Gestures must be visible to the choir.
2. Gestures must be clear and meaningful.
3. Gestures must be simple.
4. Gestures must be consistent.

Choral conductors generally do not use a baton. This is best for precision work such as in an instrumental ensemble, where the players must be able to see a clear *ichtus*, or beat. Hands are generally adequate for choral ensembles. However, this is a choice for the conductor to make. Some conductors will put emphasis on maintaining a good pulse and so they vigorously practice beat patterns. Others put emphasis on the flow of the music and stylistic interpretation. Whatever the conductor's preferences, the choir must be able to understand the conductor and become one with him. After all, the choir is the conductor's instrument.

Choral conducting is an art that requires considerable practice to become fluent. Conducting starts with the conductor doing his homework on the music. Every note must be known—every word, every breath, and every phrase. The conductor must study the music thoroughly, noting the composer's wishes, the style of music, the abilities and limitations of the singers, and the potential audience. Even the intended venue will have an impact on the way the conductor guides the music. Conducting music is easily the best example of multi-tasking. Below are a few examples of basic conducting patterns, based on simple two, three, and four beat time signatures. Of course, things become more challenging when other meters (and even changing meters) are written into the music. Practice in front of a mirror to ensure that your technique is fluent and clear.

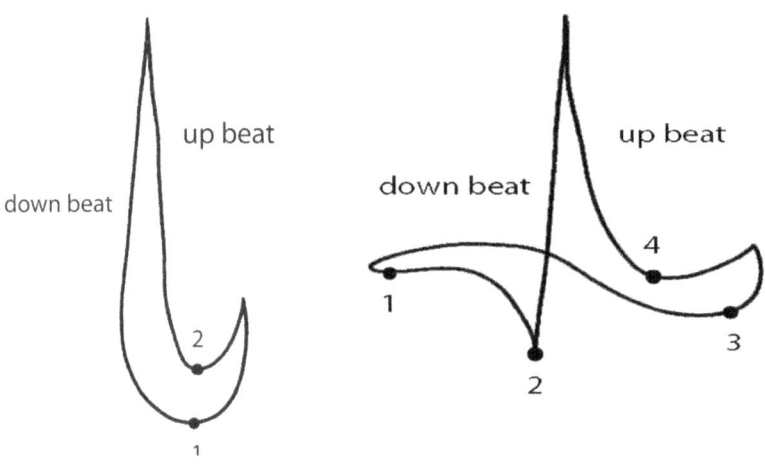

CONDUCTING PATTERNS

24 | Let Us Sing

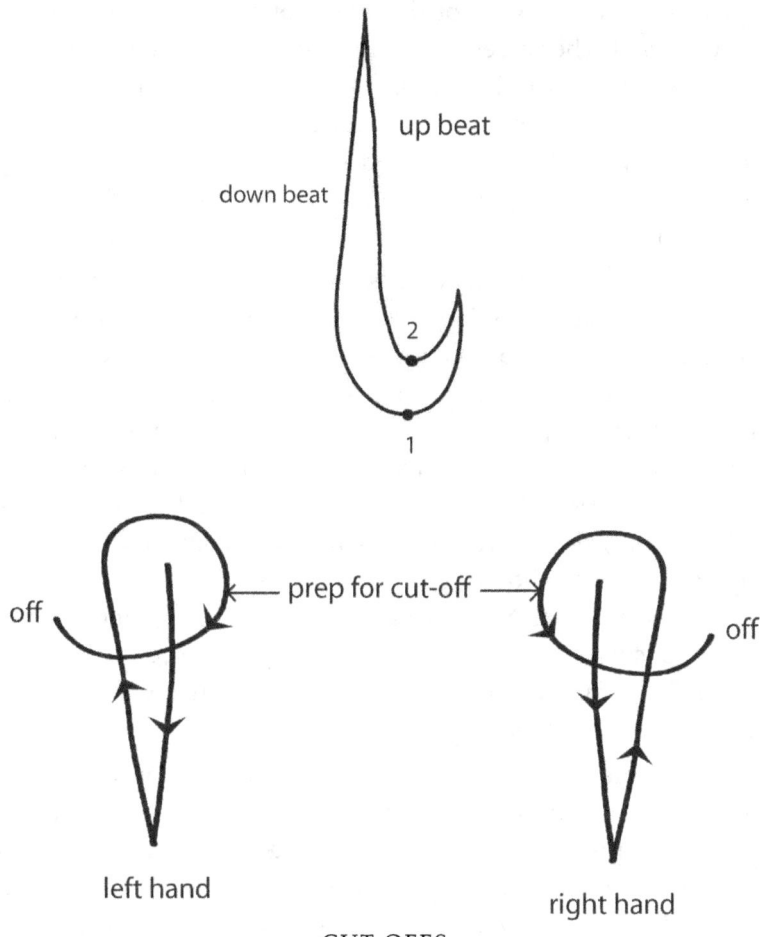

CUT-OFFS

THE TRAINER IN YOU

Few people conducting church choirs consider the fact that they are trainers. Yes, every rehearsal is a training session; yet, most directors like to believe that they are only teaching the notes to a song and when it is put together the singers will automatically do a good job. There is a reason this manual includes the origins and evolution of choral music, vocal anatomy, singing terminology, and so on. You, the director, need this information in order to know how to guide the singers. Moreover, you must impart this knowledge to the singers, or they will not grow and perform the way you want. The singers must feel and hear themselves improving. At every opportunity, explain to your singers why they must adopt good posture, why they must do the breathing exercises, and the key parts of the vocal mechanism. Occasionally, you may want to do a piece of music or a section, for no other reason than its educational benefits.

Professional choirs sometimes have vocal trainers or employ people who have professional vocal training. It is not uncommon to find choirs where half the members are paid professionals and the other half are music majors in college. The idea of professional choir members may not sit well with people whose pure religious leanings regard choir membership as a service or ministry rather than a "professional" undertaking. Indeed, most, including the choir director, do not receive any financial compensation. This may be why some choirs suffer from poor standards: There is not enough professionalism. Professional singers can enhance a choir tremendously, especially if they have the right approach. However it is not likely that someone who needs this manual will have such a choir member at their disposal.

Professionalism is not restricted to vocal performance. The choir needs to walk correctly, stand correctly, and project the correct facial expressions for the music being presented. Also, other non-musical things such as punctuality and attire play an important part in the development of professionalism. Even if your choir can never become a professional group, it is your responsibility to continuously present information and training opportunities to improve their ability to learn and perform music at a high standard. Take them to choir festivals and choral concerts, and let them see both the good and bad presentations of other groups. The internet provides a wealth of videos of choirs of every conceivable type and ability level. Make use of it. Attend training courses as often as you can. Subscribe to monthly choral music publications.

ACCOMPANIMENT

There is no doubt that choral music will require the use of musical accompaniment at various times. Personally, I prefer to teach the choir without too much accompaniment. A basic keyboard is enough. That way I can really hear what the choir is doing, and the choristers can listen to each other for a better choral tone. When the full accompaniment is added, the process of completing the music becomes much easier, and the total sound is even better.

Accompaniment must be just that—*accompaniment*. Sometimes the musicians are captured by the temptation to show how well they can play or by their enthusiasm. Accompaniment should support the singing, but must never compete with it. Today, many church choirs are supported musically by a small band—usually keyboard, drum set, bass guitar, and lead guitar, with microphones for the choir and a mixing console to control the whole thing. The microphone levels for the music will be very different to those for the choir, and the person who sits at the controls must possess the necessary sensitivity to regulate the balance between instruments and voice.

If you are fortunate enough to belong to a church where there is a good piano and, better still, a good pipe organ, then your choral repertoire will move up several notches. But be aware that good pianists and organists are not easy to find, and over enthusiasm and insensitivity to the choral group as a whole can still be an issue. Poor accompaniment is much worse than no accompaniment. Choose your music carefully so that the choir's musical abilities will be enhanced by the available instruments.

THE "P" PERSON

A choir director must be a "P" person:

Patient—Choir directors tend to be intellectual and sometimes "cannot understand why the singers can't grasp a simple concept." This job calls for patience.

Persistent—Results do not come overnight. There are many failures before success. The secret to a high-quality choir or vocal ensemble is practice, practice, and more practice!

Pleasant—Working with a choir requires a cheerful personality. You have to love working with people.

Punctual—The foundation for order in any choral group is punctuality. Insist on it.

Precise—The key characteristic which underlies every good choral director is an eye for detail. You have to see and hear everything.

Proud—Take pride in your achievements, and let the choir know that you are proud of them.

Partial—Know what you want for your choir. You can't be all things to all men and women.

Practice—Constantly practice your art to improve your techniques. There is always something new to learn.

Part Two
Practicals

Preparing the Score Notes

*"Perseverance is not one long race.
It is many short races, one after another."*
Walter Elliott

In this section, I will give examples of how you could go about analyzing various types of music for preparation to teach the choir. You can use this approach as a guide, but eventually you must develop your own approach to suit your group and circumstances. These techniques are designed for those directors who have challenges due to the limited musical abilities of their choir members. Commence the rehearsal with some kind of warm-up which will prepare the choir for the specific challenges of the music. This could be special pitch ranges, rhythmic construction, vowels, staccato sections, long sustained notes, and so on.

"DING DONG! MERRILY ON HIGH,"
arr. by Charles Wood

This is a very popular Christmas carol. A carol is a song with a religious impulse that is simple, popular, and often hilarious. Carol literature is rich in folk poetry. The carol has a dance origin and the word initially meant "to dance in a circle." It is thought that the earliest carol originated around the fifteenth century.

"Ding dong! merrily on high" is a typical example of a carol. The language of the text is early English poetry, so a brief session of reading to get the flow of the text should be done. Special attention should be paid to lightly rolling the "r" in merrily and also the tie across the phrase from "high" to "in heav'n" in verse one as well as verse three. Note the vowel colors and pronunciation used in the Latin words, "Gloria in excelsis." Be careful not to put too much "o" in "Glo-ria." Too much of a flat tongue and the "o" becomes "ah" as in "fa-ther." A relaxed jaw will solve the problem. "Excelsis" should be pronounced 'ek-shell-sis' (Roman pronunciation) with emphasis on the "shell." This carol requires a light tone and "bright eyes" for its successful delivery. Dynamically, I suggest that verse two be done at *piano-forte* level, with a crescendo on the words, "steeple bells be swungen" and "priest and people sungen."

Breath challenges in the "Gloria" can be overcome through proper posture and initial breath for the attack. A light "h" before the "o" in "Gloria," will help to avoid a sloppy run in the soprano line. Practice some staccato exercises with the choir and get them to bounce on the notes in a really light but fluid manner. However, if there remains a challenge in the breath management of the soprano line, then have the sopranos breathe after the first dotted crochet in bar three and again at bar five.

Begin the rehearsal by first teaching the verses to the soprano line, encouraging the singers to memorize the words. Next, teach the altos, one verse at a time, adding the sopranos to reinforce them each time. Go over the verses several times with just the sopranos and altos until the lines are confident. Then add the tenors, and last of all the basses—following the same pattern. Again, go over the verses several times with everyone, including the dynamic nuances which you will want at performance time. Follow the same pattern with the teaching of the "Gloria" section. The average church choir will be able to learn this piece with only a half hour of rehearsal. A really difficult group will need two or more rehearsals. Keep a moderate tempo (*andante*). If the tempo is too slow, it loses its joyfulness. If it is too fast, it will become a battle.

Ding dong! merrily on high

Words by
G. R. Woodward (1848-1934)

16th-century French melody
harmonized by Charles Wood (1866-1926)

LORD, FOR THY TENDER MERCY'S SAKE
by Richard Farrant

This beautiful a capella motet is written for soprano, alto, tenor, and bass. It is set in the key of A-flat, but you can go up or down a half-tone depending on how the sound fits your taste. I find that the lower pitch gives a very full-bodied tone whereas the A-flat gives a somewhat transparent sound, particularly if the sopranos and tenors sing with a light open tone. The basses need to be careful as they negotiate some of the low notes which need to be firm but gentle. I prefer to drop the pitch.

The text is prayerful, and correct pronunciation is a must, since the tempo is somewhat slow. Ensure that the vowel colors are correct across the choir. This piece requires good breath control from the choir because there are several places where long high notes will be required to be done with control, in order to maintain the mood of the music—for example, sopranos bars eleven to thirteen, "and incline to virtue," tenors and basses bars thirteen to sixteen, "that we may walk," also the wonderful, progressive, and expanding "Amen." The basses need to be very smooth and controlled. The trick to bringing out the beauty of this piece of music lies in the proper execution of the *messa di voce* technique.

Warm up the choir with a set of breath control exercises and stretching. Also, practice the *messa di voce* technique with chords, A-flat being one of them. Let the choir recite the text to become familiar with the flow and pronunciation of the words. Mark the breathing spots. Rehearse your conducting technique in a mirror and see if it conveys what you want. Arcs and curls in your pattern will convey the *legato* style needed. This is a piece which will require you to teach one phrase at a time. You could start with the sopranos as usual, but I think the basses should be your next line. Good pitch accuracy is required in this piece of music. Therefore, the basses and sopranos must be in tune.

Lord, for Thy Tender Mercy's Sake

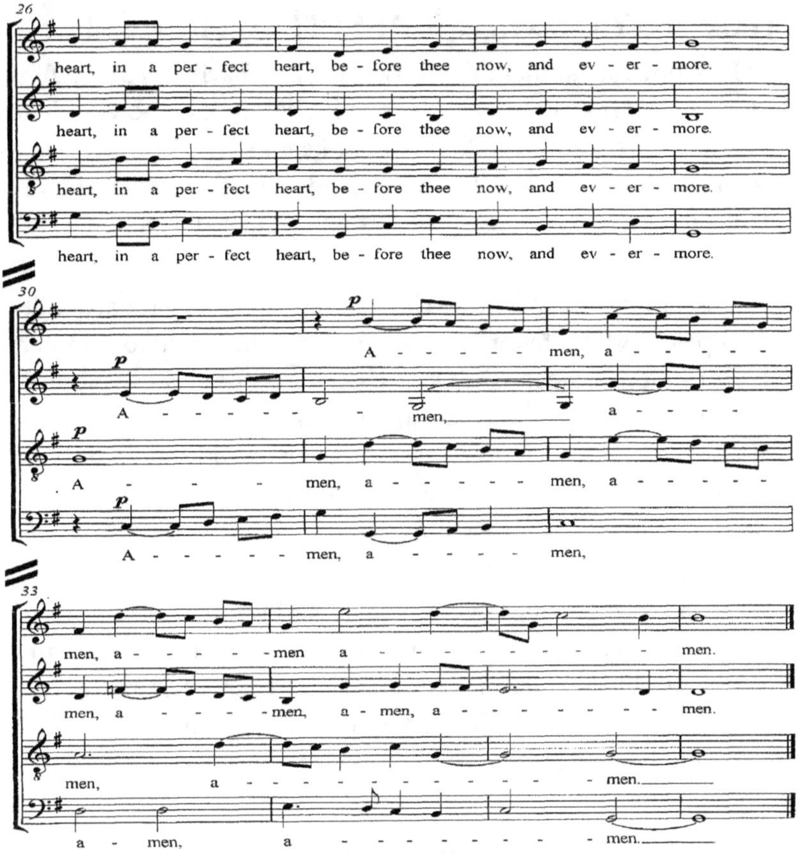
26
heart, in a per - fect heart, be - fore thee now, and ev - er - more.
heart, in a per - fect heart, be - fore thee now, and ev - er - more.
heart, in a per - fect heart, be - fore thee now, and ev - er - more.
heart, in a per - fect heart, be - fore thee now, and ev - er - more.
30
p
A - - - - - - men, a - - - - - -
A - - - - - - - men, a - - - - -
A - - - men, a - - - - - - men, a - - - - - -
A - - - - - - men, a - - - - - men,
33
men, a - - - - - men a - - - - - - - - - - - men.
men, a - - - - - men, a - men, a - - - - - - - - men.
men, a - - - - - - - - - - - - - men.
a - men, a - - - - - - - - - - men.

"JESU, JOY OF MAN'S DESIRING" by J. S. Bach

This popular anthem composed by J. S. Bach (1685–1750), is a simple but appealing piece. Its simplicity makes it accessible to amateur choirs, and yet its light, flute-like musical accompaniment gives it an air of sophistication which puts it into the ranks of more serious music. This classical piece is almost as iconic as the "Hallelujah Chorus."

The soprano and alto lines carry the essence of the tonal quality of this piece. A light tenor and bass section is sufficient to complete the choral side of the music. Of course, this is one of those pieces of music where a really good accompanist is essential to carry off the presentation. If an organ is chosen, the registration should be light, and the tempo should be moderate. Rehearse the choir's breathing with the organist so that the flow is natural.

The choir should recite the words and get a feel for the stately flow of the text. The highlight of the music occurs between bars 40 and 49. Here, confident bass and alto lines are a must. The three meter count in this piece makes it easy for even a beginning conductor to flex his muscles, but attention must be paid to the breath upstroke when cueing the choir, and also the cut-off at the end of each phrase.

Some conductors perform the two verses written for this piece, but unless there is a time issue, it is not usually necessary to do so. However, if you have access to the German words for the second verse, then it would be a good treat to do that verse in German. An amateur choir will feel like professionals when they can properly deliver Bach's "Jesu, joy."

Jesu, Joy of Man's Desiring
from Cantata No. 147 *Herz und Mund und That und Leben*

translated by Robert Bridges
(1844–1930)

J. S. Bach
(1685–1750)
edited by H. P. Allen

40 | Let Us Sing

44 | Let Us Sing

"COUNT YOUR BLESSINGS" by Edwin Excell

This is a simple folk hymn. The lyrics tell of the benefits of God's blessings and how, despite difficulties, we should still appreciate our circumstances. The tune is simple, and the harmony very accessible. The tenors and basses will find that this is an easy song to learn. Similarly, the soprano and alto lines are intuitive.

In order to enhance the delivery of this type of music, you could consider the following:

Verse 1: Full choir harmony at *mezzo forte* volume with full accompaniment.

Verse 2: Unaccompanied, soprano and alto sing the verse. Tenors and basses join in for the chorus along with a light accompaniment.

Verse 3: Full choir and accompaniment for the verse at volume level *mezzo forte*. The chorus could be done at *piano* at first, then repeated at *mezzo forte*.

Verse 4: Full choir and accompaniment for the verse at *forte*. Chorus should be done at *pianissimo*, at first, then repeated at *fortissimo*, observing a notable pause at the last "name them one by one." Then, observe a *ritenuto*, or temporary decrease in tempo, as the song comes to an end.

Count Your Blessings

"HALLELUJAH CHORUS" by G. F. Handel

Easily the most popular piece of choral composition today, the iconic "Hallelujah Chorus" has come to be recognized as an index of the choral prowess of the church choir. The majesty and pomp of this piece, coupled with its fairly accessible harmony, make it the ideal music for boosting any church choir's confidence. Many amateur choir directors no doubt would regard the successful performance of "Hallelujah Chorus" as an indication that they have "arrived."

Handel wrote this piece as part of a greater work, the *Messiah*, in 1675. The general tone is one of jubilant celebration. This means that the choir has to be large enough to provide the sound presence required. A small group of about twenty singers could make an impression provided the voices are well-trained and the accompaniment is sensitive enough. As conductor, you will need to do your homework on this piece. Practice the conducting gestures; note the possible areas of difficulty for the choir. Note the areas where expression will be needed. Decide on the tempo and dynamics.

Though the texture of the harmony is homophonic in many places, there are several sections where a bit of *fugue* is written. The best approach is to proceed line by line and add the voice parts layer by layer. The choir will have to get a good grasp on counting. For some of your singers, it may be a good idea to spend some time revising or sharpening their note counting ability. At least get them to count the time measure for each bar leading up to the entry of a new section for their voice part. Always start with the simpler voice parts in a particular section. Sometimes this will be the female voices, and sometimes it will be the male voices. Ensure that the singers follow your direction and maintain eye contact. Your conducting gestures need to be precise and predictive so that the singers can really follow you, especially at tempo changes and places where a new theme opens.

Work with the sopranos on the high notes held for eight counts at "King of Kings" and "Lord of Lords." They will need to modify the word "King" at the pitch G5, which is held for eight counts. You could use "kay-ng" in place of "king." This would facilitate the open head tone needed for the high note. It might sound funny to the sopranos, but it works. Focus on the areas where voice lines enter in a sequence. Allow the singers to grasp the sequences solidly, and then add the other lines one by one.

Finally, your accompanist will need to be able to listen to the choir and make adjustments for sections where the voices may be uncertain, such as the opening sections of "for the Lord God omnipotent reigneth." The lines enter in sequence but must subsequently follow through with a simple *fugue* which is eventually resolved at "and ever." The timing can be tricky for some.

Hallelujah Chorus

Management and the Next Generation

"The nice thing about teamwork is that you always have others on your side."
Margaret Carty

At the opening section of this manual, I alluded to the fact that a choir director at times has to wrestle with opinions and committees which try to direct the musical aspects of the choir by remote control. This problem only can be overcome if the people who choose to become involved with the choir are committed to the idea that the choir director is the expert who deals with the musical matters and everyone else deals with the non-musical matters.

That being said, it must be recognized that the choir cannot function with just the choir director alone. Every successful choir needs a management team. In the case of the church choir, that team will most likely be drawn from the choir itself, augmented with a select few from the congregation. A high school choir or junior school choir will need the support and input of the principal and, ideally, a few committed parents.

At its most basic form, the choir's management committee could be structured as follows:

1. Choir director: handles music, recruitment, repertoire, and training
2. Secretary: handles records, logistics, programs, and uniforms
3. Treasurer: Handles income and expenditures

4. Head chorister/choir leader: Handles attendance, performance assembly, assists the choir director with discipline
5. Public relations oOfficer: Coordinates the choir's activities, promotions, events, and liaisons with stakeholders

Depending on the size and activity level of the choir, these areas of responsibility could be expanded or contracted.

The choir is primarily about singing. Invariably, the production of good singing will need support resources which no choir director alone can provide. Unfortunately, most church choirs operate with an autonomous choir director as its only structural pillar. And, of course, onlookers wonder why the choir isn't developing. The greatest blight against most struggling church choirs is that there is no one properly trained to carry on the work in the absence of the established choir director or organist. Part of the reason is that the church is not taking advantage of available choral music programs to develop the potential, both within and outside of the choir. Often the excuse is lack of funding.

School choirs should serve as a nursery for the development of leadership potential in the children. The Royal School of Church Music has a chorister training scheme which is geared toward this objective. A system of training and graduation to higher and higher levels allow the children to feel and see the results of their efforts in a positive way, thus reinforcing the old model of "hard work and acceptance of responsibility results in achievement of goals."

Another reason for failing to develop existing potential is that few people are trained externally to fill this important role, and fewer still are willing to work with the minimal compensation which is offered to most directors. It is a marvel to me that the value of the choir director is placed so low on the scale. Unless you happen to be the choral director in a mega-church which has a multimillion dollar budget, you can forget about making a living from choir directing. You will be lucky to just get by.

Choir directing is a specialized skill. The choir is a special part of the body of the church and a pivotal element in the life of a school. We deliberately must set out to develop those within this body who show the talent, aptitude, and commitment for leading a choir, so that they can one day pick up the baton. They will need basic keyboard training, conducting training, vocal training, and specialized choral music training. This manual is merely providing a little introductory assistance for the budding choir director so that you will be encouraged to go further.

Microphone Placement and Use

Today, many churches rely on the use of amplified sound to enhance their worship. This is normally not a problem, and there are some well-tuned systems available which give the acoustic ambience of a large concert hall. In this case, the singers generally do not have to put much into projecting their voice. However, bear in mind that there are several pieces of electronic instrumentation "competing" with the voices. The vocal elements sometimes seem to be in competition with the accompaniment because the placement and tuning of the microphones is often incorrect. Microphones are used so often that it is easy to overlook the fact that there are right and wrong ways to use them. The greatest challenge is that persons who perform with a microphone sometimes forget that the amplified sound is affected by movement and the microphone's proximity to their mouth as well as whether or not the microphone is on axis with the sound from their mouth.

The best microphone to use for a choir is the condenser type choir microphone. These are omni-directional cardiod pattern units, which will capture several singers within a wide range. Usually, the range of pick-up for these microphones is much greater than that of even high-quality conventional unidirectional microphones; of course they are much more expensive. The choir microphone must be placed about three feet above the heads of the group and four or five feet in front of the first row of singers. This way, both the sound of the voices and the ambient acoustics of the environment will be captured. The choral sound will be heard. In an average church, choirs sitting in choir stalls usually sit in three or four rows; in this case, two microphones will be needed, and they should be spaced about six to eight feet apart.

When recording the choir, the omni-directional microphone is always the best choice for a choral ensemble. However, there is a saying that goes, "The more microphones, the more problems." If two microphones can successfully capture the sound, then do not use three. Indeed, if one microphone can properly capture the choral sound in the acoustics of the building, then that will be enough. One drawback with omni-directional microphones is that their high sensitivity makes them susceptible to feedback. Care has to be taken with the level adjustments.

The use of unidirectional microphones for choir work is to be avoided. These types of microphones are designed for solo voice work, such as a speech or when there is a single performer, small group, or for instruments. In the choir setting, the sound that is picked up will be limited to people who are directly within the sound axis of the microphone (usually no more than a foot or so spread at a distance of a foot and a half from the microphone). Obviously, capturing the sound of the full choral ensemble would be impossible with this type of microphone, unless one could use as many microphones as there are singers.

Small groups—quartets, octets, etc.—that are able to use one microphone for each voice (or even where two voices share a microphone) can successfully utilize the unidirectional microphone. But a lot still depends on the tuning provided by the control technician. The microphone should be tuned so that the singer can produce sound with ease. There should be a bit of acoustic space tuned in so that the voice can resonate in the building without being overly amplified. Test the sound with the singers in place and, having settled on a sound which suits you, note the settings on the mixing console.

Part Three
Vocalization

Basic Vocal Anatomy

"Quality is never an accident.
It is always the result of intelligent effort."
John Ruskin

Our study of choral singing will commence with a brief look at the broad instrument of singing. The human voice as a musical instrument is comprised of the whole body. Unlike a hand-held musical device, which can be put away when the performance is done, our voices are intrinsic and vital parts of our everyday existence. We are our voice. However, the exact production and manipulation of vocal tone resides in a few discrete organs and areas of the upper body, which can be described as vocal organs. For the purpose of this book, we can identify four broad areas of the vocal anatomy which have a direct bearing on voice and, consequently, on singing ability. They are respiration, phonation, resonation, and articulation.

Respiration

The lungs capture and contain air when we inhale. There are two lobes which make up the lungs. They lie on the left and right within the *thoracic cavity*, or *thorax*. Each is comprised of minute air sacs, or *alveoli*, surrounded by capillary blood vessels which enable the exchange of oxygen for the primary function of respiration. However, the secondary function of singing is enabled by the fact that the air sacs are able to contain a volume of air, much like the Scotsman's bagpipes are powered by the air contained in the air bag. The nostrils are the external ports through which air enters the lungs. Air also enters via the mouth when needed in large or

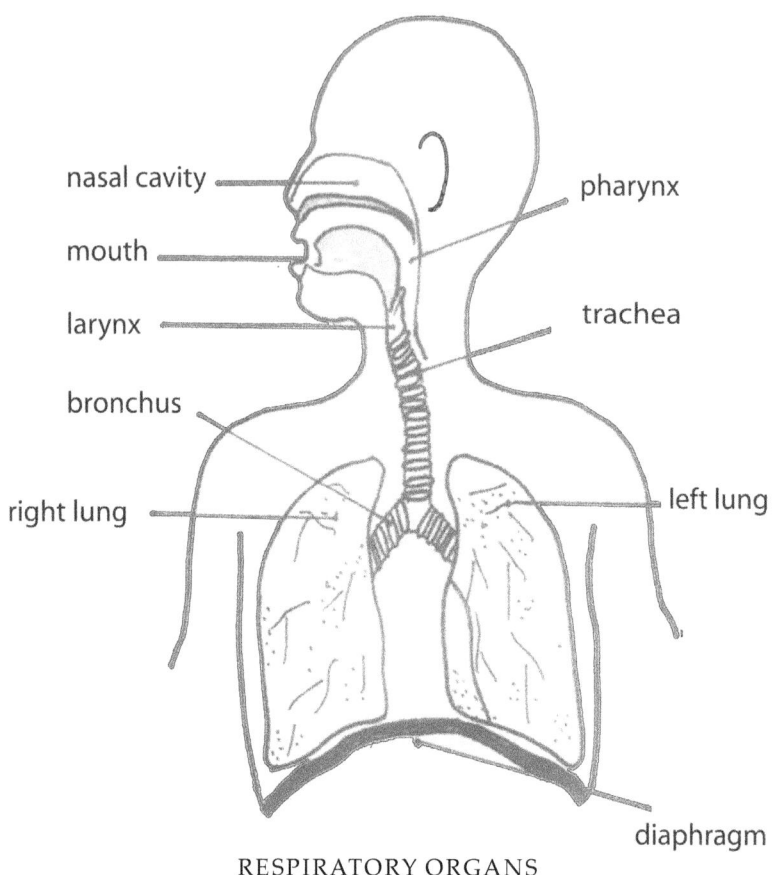

RESPIRATORY ORGANS

sudden volume. The air is directed down through the *trachea* and to the lungs. The ribcage provides the structural support for anchoring the thoracic muscles and protecting the lungs and heart. The ribs are manipulated by the thoracic muscles. *Intercostals* and *ceratus* muscles raise and lower the thoracic cavity during inhalation and exhalation. Other muscles in the back assist with spinal support for the thorax.

Last but not least, is the *diaphragm*, a muscular sheet of tissue separating the thoracic organs from those in the abdomen. The diaphragm is shaped somewhat like an open umbrella, with the dome extending upward into the thoracic region. The diaphragm is often described as the foundation of breathing. It provides the

vacuum pressure that sucks air into the lungs. Inhalation occurs when the muscles in the diaphragm compress, causing it to move downward. Externally, the action of the diaphragm can be seen as the compression and relaxation of the *epigastrum*, an area of muscles below the base of the sternum where the ribs meet above the abdominal muscles. This action is clearest when observing a person breathing while lying on their back.

Respiration is supported by the skeleton. It is very important that singers adopt proper posture when performing, because the lungs and diaphragm are activated by muscular action which can be quite demanding. A properly aligned frame provides a good anchor for the muscles. Excessive movement while singing is not a recommended technique for good choral tone, as it interferes with breath control. Even in musical theatre and opera the performers measure the extent of their movements to achieve a reasonable balance between the vocal and visual requirements.

Phonation

The *larynx*, otherwise known as the voice box, is a small valve comprised of muscles, skin tissue, and cartilage, and is located in the throat. Externally, we recognize its position in males as the "adam's apple." The larynx has two horizontal strips of delicate tissue described as "cords" or "folds," which oscillate when air is passed through them in a particular way. The passage from the throat, or *pharynx*, to the larynx, is guarded by a flap of cartilage at the base of the tongue, called the *epiglottis*. This flap closes off the entrance to the trachea when we swallow, so that food and other particles do not enter the lungs. The vocal folds have a special mucous lining which needs to be constantly moist in order to function correctly. The folds are manipulated by small vocal muscles attached to pieces of cartilage.

Resonation

In the study of physics, *resonance* is a condition where vibrations or pulses generated by a source (sound, electricity) are impacted on a receiver (usually some other physical material) in such a manner that the vibrations approach the natural vibration frequency of the impacted material. As the intensity of this vibra-

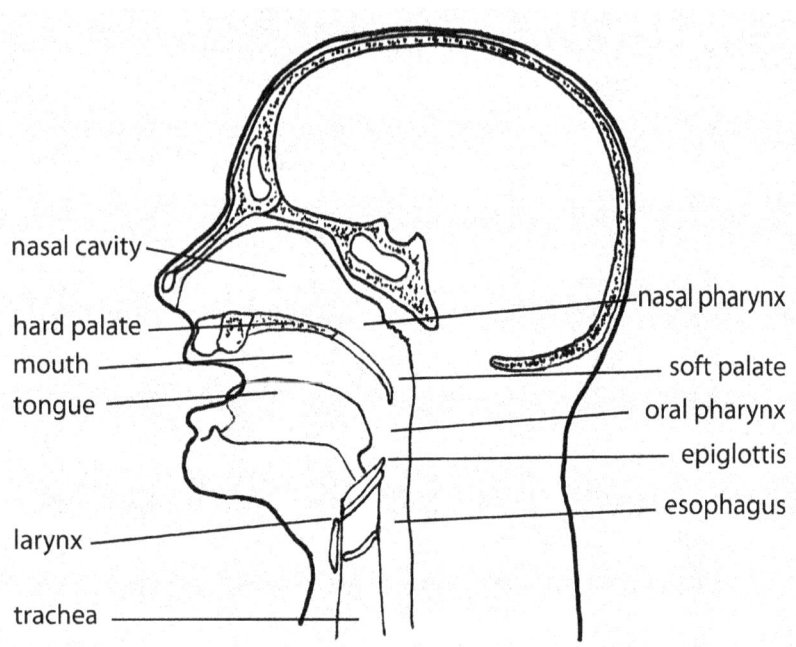

RESONATORS AND ARTICULATORS

tion increases, the amplitude of the response grows exponentially. In the case of the operatic soprano who is able to break the wine glass by singing, the frequency of her vocal pitch mimics the natural resonant frequency of the wine glass material; by intensifying her vocal production she is able to increase the vibration amplitude of the glass, overwhelm the physical integrity of the glass, and shatter it.

The vocal areas that we identify as resonators are the mouth cavity, nasal cavity, and throat. These resonators respond to our generated tone so that the sound is amplified and we become aware of a definite response (sympathetic vibration) in a particular area of our body. Fortunately, we won't shatter any body parts like the wine glass. However, this phenomenon enables us to speak of "head tone," "chest tone," and "mask resonance."

The nature of the response can be controlled directly by the singer to some degree; however, there is a significant aspect of indirect manipulation. It is for this reason that singing is sometimes difficult to explain. The sensations vary from person to person. Nevertheless, singers can learn to increase the resonant response in various areas of the body by practicing particular exercises. Care of the resonators requires care of the body as a whole. Adequate exercise, rest, and good nutrition will ensure that the resonators function properly.

The identification of resonators in various areas of the body gives rise to the concept of "voice placement." The perceived effects of resonance in diverse areas of the body allows us to use our voice in a much more effective and targeted way when singing. An untrained person can have a naturally beautiful voice simply because they have a predisposition to sing with a particular resonant placement which gives rise to a nice tone. However, it is possible to improve the tone by deliberately encouraging certain resonant placements. In this way, a singer could develop a good pharyngeal muscle tone and enhance the beauty of his/her vocal tone.

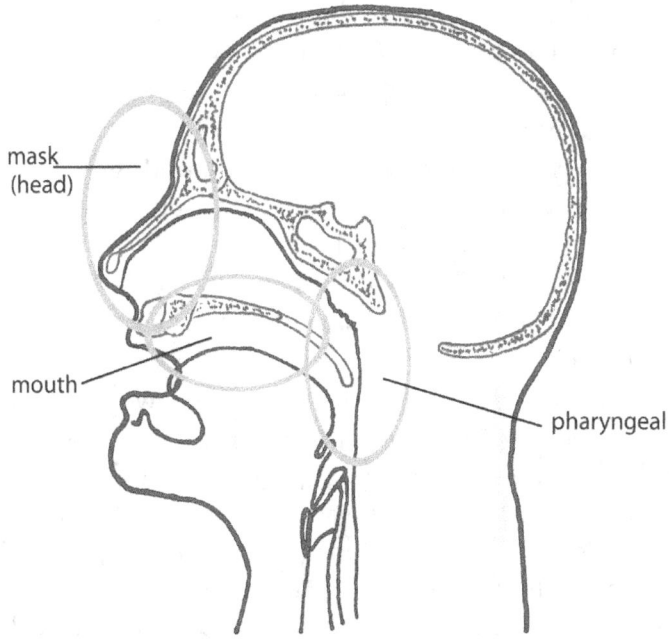

RESONANCE PLACEMENT

A good choir is able to sing in such a manner that the very building in which it is performing resonates with the singers' tones, amplifies the singing, and even introduces non-vocal sounds. The *acoustics* of a building also affect the choir's tone. For example, a choir singing in a building made with marble floors, walls, and columns can produce a very clear ringing tone. The same choir will sound quite different when singing in a building which has carpeted floors and several open windows. The worst acoustic environment is actually outdoors. It takes practice to make a good choral sound outdoors. Barbershop quartets have a special sound brought about by the way the chords are written. In fact, when very skilled singers perform four-part harmony, a fifth voice can be heard which produces the characteristic "barbershop" sound.

Articulation

Articulators include teeth, lips, tongue, palate, and jaw. They enable us to understand the text of the music. I use the term "music" to describe not just the words and notes on a paper, but also the voice itself. Articulators modify and interrupt the tone to form words even while the music is flowing from the voice.

The teeth create crisp consonants. A slight "smile on the tone" will brighten the sound. Professional singers know that a smiling face not only looks good, it also sounds good. However, too much teeth can adversely affect the tone. The lips shape the opening of the mouth and need to be employed with a light action. Too much lip covering the teeth will result in a dull tone. Again, if the teeth are exposed too much, you can end up with a strident tone.

The tongue is an unruly member! Without it we could say very little, let alone sing. The tongue has a marked impact on tone and vowels. A common problem among untrained singers is a tongue that tends to stay high and spread in the mouth. This makes for a very unpleasant "bleating" tone (try imitating a goat), reduces the volume of the resonating space in the mouth, and distorts the vowels. For some singers, controlling the tongue is a challenge. Generally, the tongue needs to be relaxed, but flexible to respond

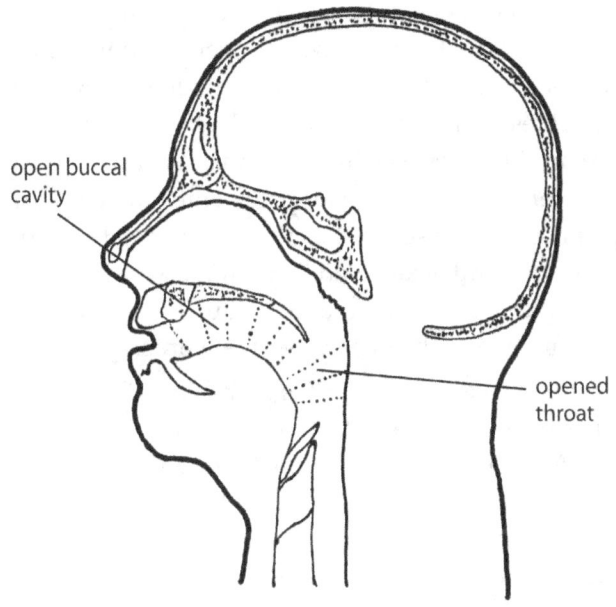

LOW TONGUE POSITION

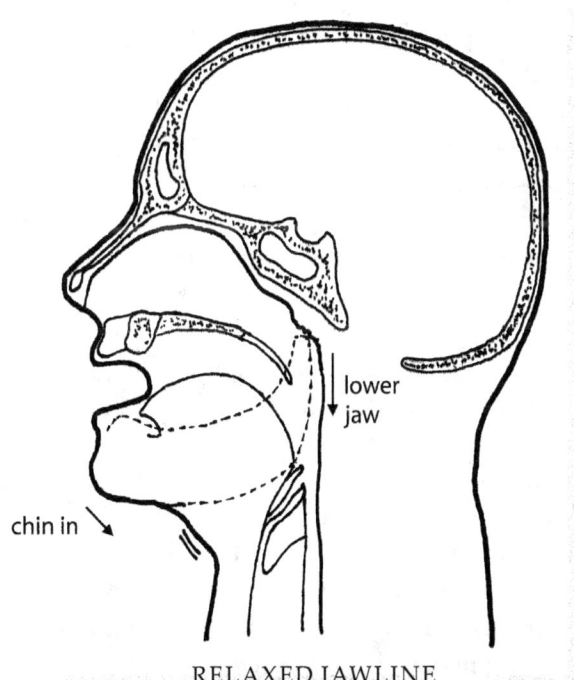

RELAXED JAWLINE

Basic Vocal Anatomy | 73

to vowel-shape needs as the music and text requires. Our tongue determines our speech accent, so it is very important to understand the position and function of the tongue in vowel formation and tone. Professional singers have to learn to control how their vowels are produced, especially if the music is in foreign language. Tongue twisters can help to develop flexibility and coordination in our tongue use. Try these: "red leather, yellow leather," or "black background, brown background." Say these words out loud at a slow, deliberate speed at first, and gradually improve the speed while still maintaining the integrity of the words.

The jaw allows expansion of the *buccal* (mouth) cavity and the *pharynx* (upper throat area). The jaw must be relaxed and flexible at all times. A low jaw facilitates a low larynx, and consequently, an open pharynx, which is a cornerstone of healthy vocal production. All the articulators (teeth, lips, tongue, palate, and jaw) have to be coordinated to produce music and words simultaneously.

There are two other key parts of the body that are as important to singing as any of the others—the ears and the brain. They are the mechanisms of feedback, control, and artistic engagement. Many people who possess a naturally good voice are challenged by intonation difficulties, because the feedback loop is flawed. I find that this is by far the most common problem that many singers and choir directors encounter. Solutions to this problem are most effective when persons are younger rather than older. Vocal concepts such as resonance and placement require a mind which can self-analyze. These concepts are not tangible in the physical sense. It helps greatly when you, the director, are able to demonstrate the concepts and understand the difficulties which your students encounter as you attempt to teach the techniques. Singing is rather like walking. When a toddler is learning to walk, its mind has to learn to control the muscles which maintain an upright position, while positioning the legs in the actual walk. Although aspects of the action are deliberate, much of the skill of walking comes about by the brain learning to use the feedback loop from the muscular nerves and the balance mechanism of the ears. One could never teach a toddler to walk simply by explaining these concepts to him/her. Therefore, teaching the concept of singing is best done by showing.

In summary, singers need to be aware of the processes and body systems which are involved in singing. The best advice I can give to any budding singer is to practice making pleasant tones and avoid loud, strenuous sounds. The singer must be able to picture the organs interacting, even as the singing is being done. The aspiring singer must have keenly linked ears and mind to analyze action and effect, and learn to control the interaction of all body parts involved in singing.

BREATH MANAGEMENT

> *"There is always a better way."*
> Thomas Edison

Now that we know something about the body parts used in singing, we can move on to the primary foundation of singing: *breath management*. Like every strong building structure with a solid foundation, breath management represents the foundation of good singing. Now, we must start with the skeletal support or posture. The basic posture consists of an upright stance. Imagine being held upright by a string attached to the top of your head, the weight of your body placed on the front half of your feet, your head slightly tilted downward, chin tucked in, eyes looking forward, shoulders back and relaxed, hands at the sides or in front (not behind)—it's not as difficult as it sounds! If you sit to sing, as in a rehearsal, you must sit forward on the chair with your back tall and feet flat on the ground. Proper skeletal alignment reduces the muscular effort required for breathing and, consequently, allows more energy for singing. Please keep in mind that what we are trying to achieve here is a habit of good posture. It is not the objective of this section to make you complete a checklist of items every time you contemplate singing; it must be a subconscious, reflex action.

Breath management is very important to singing. Vocal tone is initiated by breath pressure coming up from the lungs. The vocal folds close and block the passage of air from the lungs. As the air pressure builds against the closed vocal folds, a point is

imaginary string

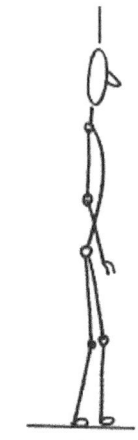

PROPER POSTURE

reached where the muscles of the folds yield and release the air in a "pop." This action repeats many times per second to create the basic "buzz" of the voice. The tightness with which the vocal muscles hold the folds against the breath pressure determines the relative frequency of the "pop" and, thus, the pitch of the tone. The same breath pressure determines the volume of the sound. Through breath management we are able to train our vocal muscles and improve the quality of our tone and pitch. Poor breath management is one of the main causes of vocal damage.

The key to good singing is breath management; not simply breathing, but managing your breath. Essentially, we want to inhale a sufficient amount of air that will allow us to produce a pleasant tone, and then support that tone at the correct pitch and volume across a musical phrase. When we inhale, we should strive for optimal capacity according to what is to be sung. Nasal breathing maintains a warming and filtering of the air, but has a limiting effect on the flow rate of air into the lungs. *Buccal*, or mouth breath-

inhaling

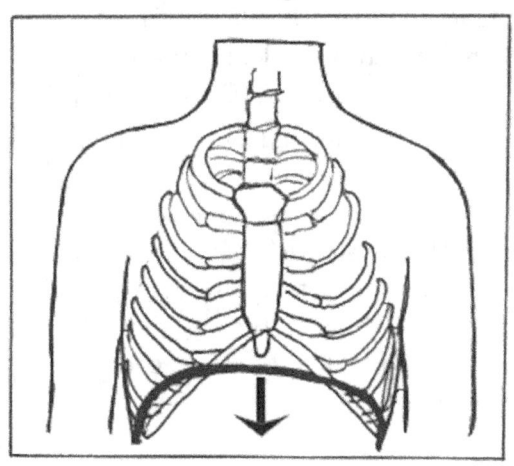

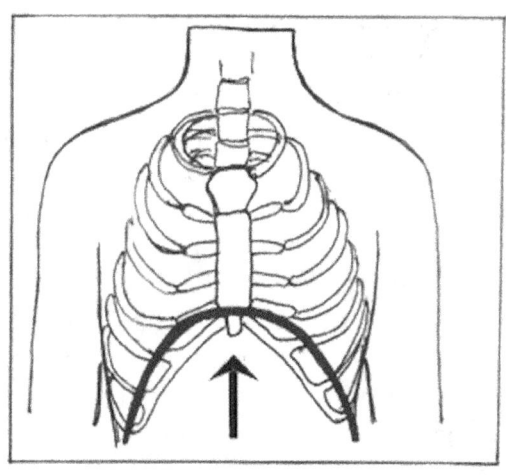

exhaling

ACTION OF THE DIAPHRAGM

ing, provides the best air flow rate but invites cold, contaminated air into the lungs and there is also the danger of partial activation of the vocal folds when inhaling through the mouth. This can damage the vocal folds. A silent inhale is preferable.

The best balance is a mixture of the two, adjusted according to the requirements of the music. The singer should strive for a relaxed flared nostril inhalation or a combination of mouth and nostril, as if experiencing a pleasant surprise. During a performance, it will become necessary to rapidly inhale and fill the lungs. In this case the singer has to learn the art of letting the air "fall" into the lungs. This is where a well-exercised diaphragm comes in.

A good choir is characterized by the smoothness and ease with which it completes the musical phrases, breathing where it counts and controlling the quality of "tonal attacks." In order to perform very long musical phrases, which may challenge the singer's breath capacity, it is sometimes necessary to "stagger" the breathing. That is, some singers should take a breath while others sing on, and while the first set sings on, the second set could take a breath. This, of course, requires rehearsal.

Young kids have underdeveloped lungs and vocal mechanisms. It is important that in giving instructions on breathing and other vocal techniques, we do not expect too much from them in terms of results. Children should not be expected to produce vocal performances which parallel adult performances. It is often seen where young children are pushed by adults to perform like high-end stars in the popular music and gospel music domains. After some time, these child stars fade from the spotlight. The main reason is that their voices have been damaged in some way and they are no longer viable as "star singers."We have to be responsible as teachers, especially when we deal with children, who do not know that there is danger in forcing their voice. To them and, of course, to the misguided adults who encourage them, they sound like real pop or gospel singers.

PHONATION, RESONATION, REGISTRATION

"If you can imagine it, you can achieve it.
If you can dream it, you can become it."
    William Arthur Ward

Phonation is the process of producing vocal tone, also called *vocalizing*. In essence, we make a basic vocal sound when air passes up through the larynx from the lungs. The *larynx* is an air valve which restricts the intrusion of foreign material into the lungs, but it also creates the sound of our voice when air passes the opposite direction. Whenever air has to pass through a hole, over an edge, or through a slot at speed, it makes a sound. All wind instruments operate on this principle, and the voice is, after all, a wind instrument. The nature of the vocal tone depends on how other aspects of our vocal tract affect it. Imagine a simple loudspeaker. If you hold it in your hand when it is playing, it is not very impressive. But, if it is installed in an enclosure such as a speaker box or your car, it comes to life. Similarly, the strings of a guitar are not effective if you merely string them between two pegs in open air and pluck them. But when the same strings are installed against the guitar's sounding board the difference is dramatic.

Without good use of his/her resonators, a singer will not be impressive. In the case of man-made wind instruments, the resonators are static, and the only thing that can be changed is the *phonator* (e.g. the position of the fingers over the holes of the flute). Our instrument (our voice) is a living thing. This makes the voice a very intricate musical instrument, united with the player. But on the other hand, that can make the adjustments all the more complicated to play properly.

We are able to adapt and improve our instrument through exercise and practice. In this way, even a mediocre singer can become much better over time. Additionally, our instrument is able to modify its resonators at will, to create a wide variety of tones. Thus, we can depict moods and colors with our tones. After producing a sound, we use our resonators to manipulate it. The following list describes the four main ways resonators may affect tone.

1. Pharynx (throat and nasal cavities)—The relaxed or open throat is essential for all voice types, but especially if you are a bass or alto, or are trying to produce rich, dark, tones. The muscles of the pharynx must be toned and flexible. This is achieved through vocal exercise using particular vowels and pitch. The open throat also allows for a low laryngeal position. A high larynx indicates muscular tightness in the pharyngeal wall which causes a constriction which in turn negatively affects the muscles of the larynx. Keeping a low larynx frees the voice and relaxes the extrinsic vocal muscles.

2. Buccal (mouth cavity)—The mouth is a variable enclosure. It can be made large or small, and by muscular manipulation it can have soft or firm walls.

3. Sinuses and nasal cavities—The sinuses provide an index of feedback on the tone because the thin nature of the bones and tissues of the sinuses make them sensitive to the vibrations produced during tone production. When these tones are produced in a certain way, the sensation is felt in the head, as if that is where the tone emanates from; this is known as "head tone." The nasal cavity amplifies the tone, and the sinuses make us aware of the tone's intensity.

4. Ears—The ears are the ultimate guide to tone. The ears tell you whether you have got it right or not. A skilled voice teacher can guide you as you practice, but if you are keen, you can help yourself by recording your choir and listening to the playback. Then, you have to make the adjustments. In addition, get a voice expert to listen to your group and give you feedback. As usual, practice, practice, practice!

Registration is a term applied to the different musculo-vocal feelings we have when we sing notes ascending from low to high or vice versa. Some voice teachers speak of a three register concept: chest, middle, head. Some speak of a two-register concept: chest and head. And yet, others speak of a concept without defined "registers." Whatever the view, every singer will notice an area of natural vocal comfort—the *modal*, or speech voice—and an area where more effort and concentration is required. The border between the two is called *passaggio*. For sopranos, the area of transition is the lower notes because sopranos sing in the higher register more often. The opposite is true for basses and baritones. In this regard, we can identify two registers: a heavy, chest voice and a light, head voice, with a transition zone (*passaggio*) in between.

Altos and tenors have to wrestle with register issues more often, as they sing in the *passagio* area more often. The reason for this problem lies in the nature of vocal production. In order to produce tone, the vocal folds must be adjusted by the vocal muscles. As with any such mechanism, there is a limit. But sometimes, the music demands an upper range of voice beyond the ability of the singer's modal voice. During modal voice production the vocal folds are in contact with each other throughout the sound cycles. Higher pitch requires firmer contact and more breath pressure. This is where the problem occurs, because the folds can withstand only so much pressure. The solution for that problem is to employ the "light vocal mechanism." This mechanism is much easier to use at a higher pitch, but requires more breath support and development of the resonators in order to have sufficient power. The light voice uses

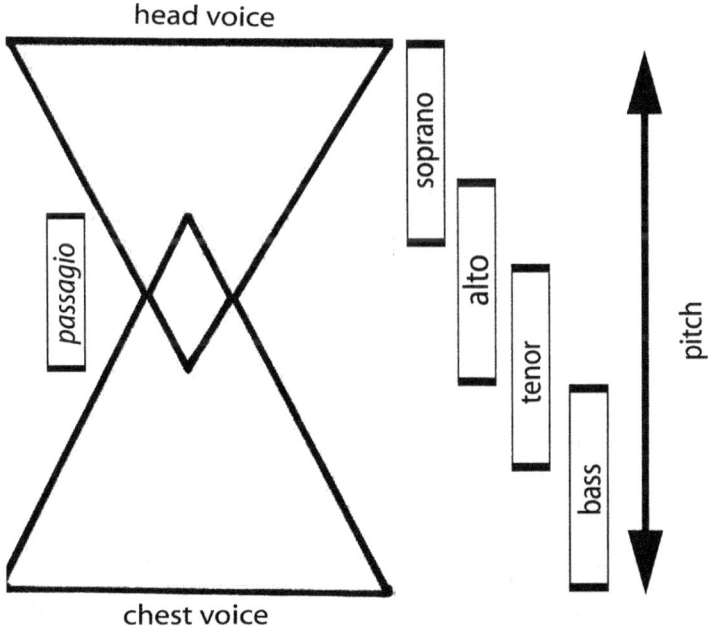

REGISTRATION HOURGLASS

Basic Vocal Anatomy | 81

thinned out vocal folds, which are actually open and vibrate along the inner edges. One has to practice good breathing techniques in order to properly support the light voice. Additionally, one should also exercise the resonators in order to develop the required amplification for the light voice. Vocal exercises which use the 'lee' and 'loo' sounds will help the development of the head voice.

A sudden change from heavy to light voice and vice versa, results in a phenomenon which is sometimes described as "yodeling." Young boys entering puberty are the best examples of this transition

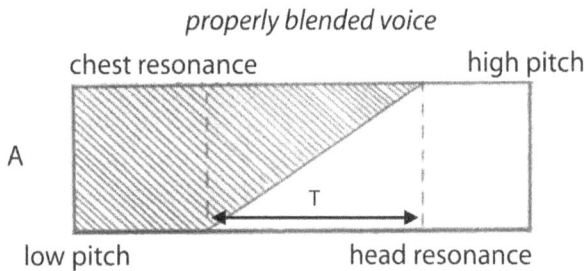

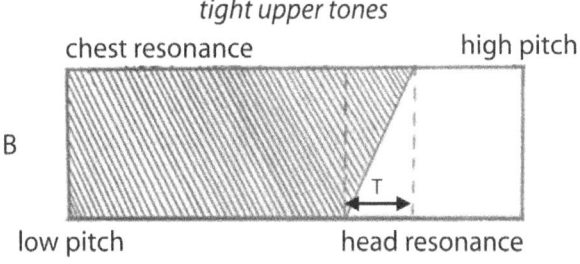

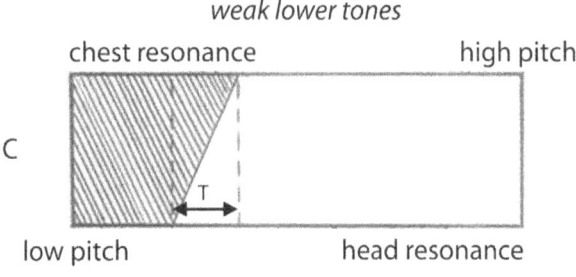

REGISTRATION TRANSITION

phenomenon. Their voice pitch undergoes a drop of up to an octave. The voice has to learn control during this period of change, as the vocal folds elongate and thicken. Sometimes the folds blow open during normal speech inflections and consequently, the boy's voice is heard yodeling. Every good singer should practice managing register changes and develop the "light mechanism," to avoid yodeling. We speak with the "heavy mechanism," and generally, this is the register with which we prefer to sing. However, the light mechanism is essential for a properly rounded and pleasant tone with good range.

A contemporary vocal style called "belting" relies on the exclusive use of the chest voice and the modal voice, without transition to a "light mechanism." In this style of singing there are high, medium, and low voice types. The traditional soprano, alto, tenor, and bass categories do not apply. The pitch hovers around alto, regardless of age or gender. The belting tone is generally characterized by loudness, shrillness, drama, intensity, emotion, and tension. One key aspect of belting is that the tone is placed in the mouth, resonating against the hard palate, with a wide mouth and stiff tongue. An important thing to note, however, is that different people have different natural vocal ranges—some may be comfortable with a certain pitch level, while others may have to put out great effort to accomplish that same pitch level.

Belting carries a lot of energy, dynamism, and intensity with it, and it is an intuitive vocal form. Eminent vocal researcher, Jo Estill, who has conducted research on the belting technique, describes the belting voice as "an extremely muscular and physical way of singing." Her observations of performers have shown that it requires the following:

- Minimal airflow compared to other types of phonation
- Maximum muscular engagement of the torso
- Engagement of muscles in the head and neck to enable stabilization of the larynx
- A downward tilt of the cricoid cartilage
- High larynx
- Maximum muscular effort of the extrinsic laryngeal muscles, minimum effort at the level of the true vocal folds.

Singers must operate in the voice range that best suits them (*tessitura*). This may or may not be the normal speech voice range, and sometimes it is only through vocal training that people "discover their voice." Male altos (counter-tenors) for example sing in a vocal range far different from their speech voice range. Through training, many learn to sing with a lower or higher voice.

Most classically trained choirs use a vocal style which relies on the generous application of the head voice, mask attack, and light chest. In the eighteenth century, *bel canto* was described as a style of singing in which emphasis was placed on making beautiful tones with the voice. Good breath support, vowel formation, and use of the resonators were emphasized. The right acoustic environment and skilled singers are a prerequisite for the performance of this style to be appreciated. All traditional church choirs should aim for a *bel canto* style production. A children's choir should be exposed to a variety of styles, but ultimately, learn and use *bel canto* as a foundation for basic production.

We can quickly define four basic voice categories: soprano, alto, tenor, and bass. Of course, there are many subcategories within these. On the pianoforte, bass is defined within the notes E2 to C4, baritone within G2 to E4, tenor within B3 to G4, alto or counter-tenor within F3 to D5, and soprano within C4 to A5. These are, of course, average range definitions. Singers will have lower or higher ranges according to their individual talent. A person should strive to develop their voice so they can comfortably sing a range of two octaves. In addition to vocal range, a singer's voice type is also defined by their vocal tone. A skilled alto could sing up to an F5, but the tone will still sound like that of an alto. The key to this development is *practice*. As a choir director, patience will be one of the greatest virtues toward your success.

INTONATION CONTROL AND ENUNCIATION

"To keep a lamp burning, we have to keep putting oil in it."

Mother Teresa

Intonation is dependent on the ear and on breath control. The best way to train the ear is by singing. Children who come from a background where singing is an everyday habit quickly develop the ability to reproduce pitch very accurately.

A skilled singer can go off pitch if breath control is faulty. Pitch is dependent on breath support, particularly for long sustained tones. This is why a singer should be in good physical condition. The solution for poor intonation is good breath control and practice, practice, practice.

In order to achieve good intonation within a choir, the director should place the stronger singers together toward the middle of the line of performers. The less-experienced singers should be at the ends. The stronger singers are reinforced by proximity to each other, and the weaker ones are placed in a position where they can hear both themselves and the stronger singers. Basses and sopranos tend to sing an octave apart, therefore optimal tuning occurs when the basses are positioned close behind the sopranos. This applies whether at rehearsal or a performance.

There is no harm in listening to a recorded example of the music which the choir is learning. This may help the group to appreciate the music as a whole and could help with intonation. However, the extensive use of recorded singing for a rehearsal is to be avoided. Singers can develop a false sense of security if they are imitating a recorded piece as part of their rehearsal. When the recording is removed, the singers struggle to maintain the music. If you use an electronic keyboard instrument for rehearsals with children, select a harp tone when playing. The harp tone tends to mimic the vocal hum in a typical head voice tone, and this can help the singers to stay on pitch.

Singing with four voice parts (SATB) poses a problem for some people because they are not readily able to distinguish between their notes and those of another close voice part, especially if they have to sing a lower part. One way to develop this ability among the singers is to have them do regular ear tests. A simple exercise involves playing two notes of a triad simultaneously on the keyboard, and then the singers identify the lower of the two pitches. With practice, they will learn to distinguish between the two notes and can reproduce the pitch of either one at will. As a followup to this test, you can do an exercise with the three notes of the triad simultaneously. The challenge then is to find the middle, lower, or upper note accurately. Choose simple two-part songs for the choir at first, and as the group's confidence builds you can introduce more challenging music. A person who is unable to reproduce pitch accurately, even after extensive tutoring, may be tone-deaf, and will require expert handling to correct this condition. If at all possible, seek the assistance of a good, experienced vocal coach to remedy the problem.

The Singer's Enunciation

"It's not knowing what to do, it's doing what you know."
Anthony Robbins

Enunciation refers to the way we shape words, which syllables are emphasized, and how we produce the consonants. If we do not shape the words correctly, both the understanding of the text and the musical quality are compromised.

Speech accents, habits, and local dialects influence how we produce our words. One aspect of enunciation is *vowel variation*. Vowel variation refers to the different tone qualities a singer produces from the same vowel. We can describe the sound of an "e" as a warm tone, as opposed to an "a" or an "i," which are bright tones. Some vowels are placed forward in the mouth, while others are formed in the rear. The pharynx, tongue, and lips are used to shape the vowels, and we can see how, for example, the height of the tongue affects the placement of the vowel, as shown in the diagram on page 87.

Choral music generally has a text. The composer structures the music bearing in mind the text—not just the words, but also the meaning. In a sense, the composer is painting a work of art using words and sounds on a canvas, the setting in which the singing is to take place. In order to fully appreciate the composer's intentions, the choir must be in tune with this background. Every singer has a duty to know something about the music being performed to do a good job, and it is the director's duty to explain it.

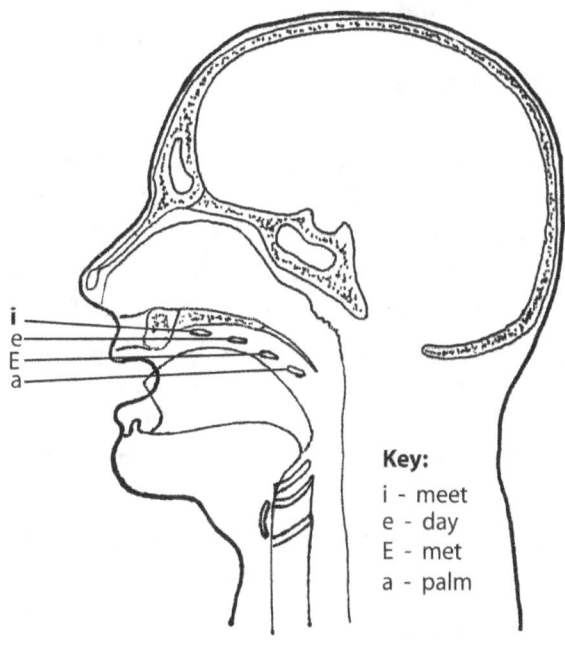

VOWEL PLACEMENT

Giovanni da Palestrina was a sixteenth century composer, famed for his ability to compose polyphonic music with startling beauty. He had a thorough understanding of the human voice, its possibilities and limitations. He was able to compose around vowels as a center-point for the notes and chords. To perform Palestrina's music in anything other than the original language (Latin) would disregard the composer's creative genius, and destroy the innate beauty of his music. The words are important.

When we speak, we produce words in a different way than when we sing. Singing is about sustaining tone on the vowels. The sung vowel is an acoustic production. Thus, the vowel is king when we sing. Time must be set aside to practice the correct pronunciation of vowels. One good way to do this is to let the singers read the text aloud, observing the poetic interpretations. A good technique for unearthing bad pronunciation and undesirable dialect habits, is to read the words aloud, very slowly, syllable by syllable. An important thing to remember is that when a choir sings all the members must enunciate—produce the words and sounds—similarly.

Persons from different countries will naturally tend to pronounce words differently because of dialect differences. In fact, even within the same area of a country there are differences in dialect. It is up to the choir director to hear the differences and take steps to unify them. Dialect is the result of speech habits which began when we were very young. Usually, we are not aware of our own dialect, but we can readily hear someone else's dialect. Dialect results from muscular habits in our tongue position and lips in particular. Sometimes these habits can be a challenge to undo.

The International Phonetic Alphabet gives a guide to the correct pronunciation of vowels as it relates to singing:

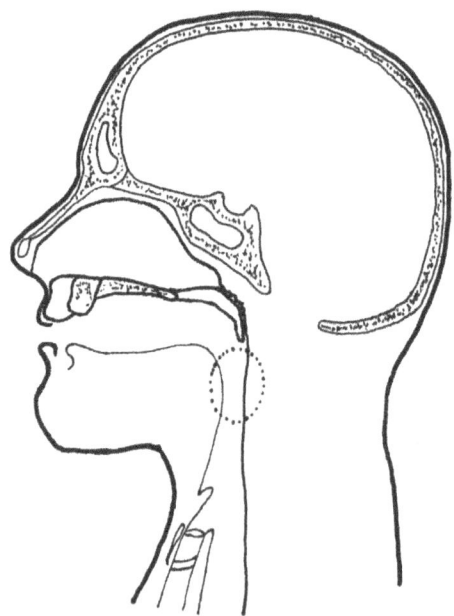

PLACEMENT FOR "AH" (A)

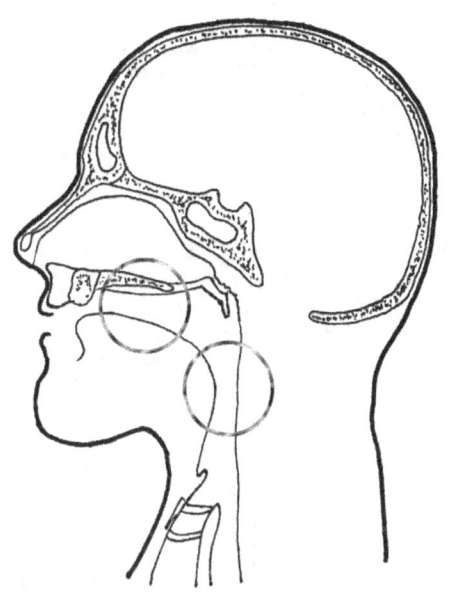

PLACEMENT FOR "AY" (E)

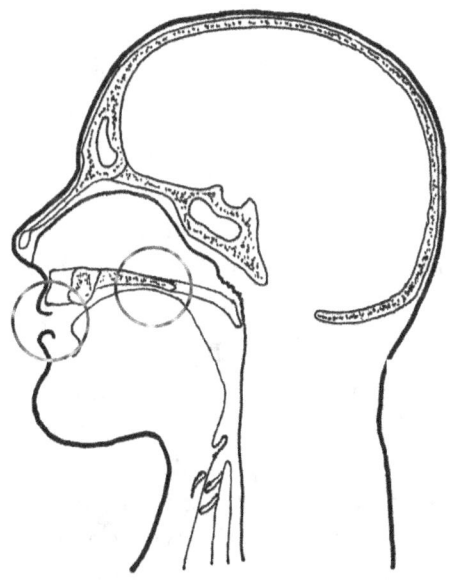

PLACEMENT FOR "E" (I)

Basic Vocal Anatomy | 89

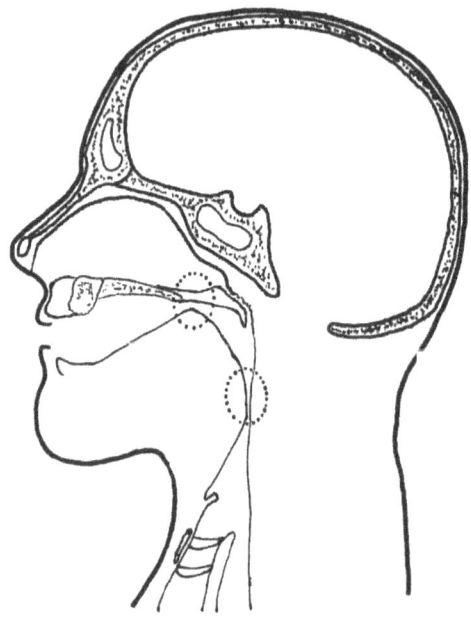

PLACEMENT FOR "OO" (U)

Here are two examples of how to correctly pronounce commonly sung words:

1. "God": The "o" should be sung with an open mouth and a relaxed jaw, as in "of," but do not overemphasize the "aw" sound. Some singers pronounce the "o" with a wide mouth and it comes out "gahd." In this case, the tongue is too high and the lips are too horizontal.

2. "Glory": The "o" should be sung as in "snow" and the "ry" as in the "ri" in "rift." "glo-ry," not "glah-ray."

Dipthongs refer to two adjacent vowel sounds occurring within the same syllable. Several two syllable words require emphasis on the first syllable only. For example, in "mighty" the emphasis often is placed on the second syllable, but it should be sung with emphasis on the first syllable. Single syllable words ending in a consonant tend to be rushed, and there is a tendency to place extra emphasis on the last consonant; "us" should be sung "uh-s," with a slight break before the "s." "Let" should be sung "leh-t," with a slight break before the "t."

There are three ways to pronounce an "r":

 a. The American style "r," as in "run," "rip," and "river." The front of the tongue is up and curled back, lips pursed

 b. The Spanish style "r" as in "puerto." The tip of the tongue flutters against the hard palate.

 c. The Caribbean style "r" as in, "person," pronounced "peuson." The front of the tongue is rolled laterally, and the lips are slightly pursed. This is a good way to avoid pronouncing the "r" when it occurs in the middle of a word.

Words ending with an "r" should be sung with the Caribbean style "r," and words beginning with an "r" should be sung with the Spanish style "r." The American style "r" is used in instances when the "r" is not prominent, as in "brother," "America," and "praise." When a singer attempts to sing very high notes, the voice becomes unable to form vowels in a normal way, which distorts the words. However, the trained voice will recognize this as an opportunity for vowel modification. As the pitch rises, so does the effort to maintain speech-vowel identity. The sound volume falls off, and in order to maintain reasonable vocal tone and volume, the jaws and pharynx open, the soft palate arches, and all of the vowels morph into an "ah" sound. Lyric sopranos are very familiar with this phenomenon.

It helps in normal range singing to realize that higher notes require vowel modification in order to maintain good delivery. The skilled singer will know to add a little openness gradually to the tone as the pitch rises. The audience will not hear the change when it is done properly. The text should be understandable, even with pitch challenges. This is the singer's job. Success is measured by the degree to which the singer is able to integrate all aspects of vocal production to make music.

Taking Care of Your Voice

"The successful man will profit from his mistakes and try again in a different way."
Dale Carnegie

The human voice is unique. It is one of the most valuable attributes we possess. From the time we are born until we die, our voice defines us. Yet, we often take for granted that we can simply open our mouths and out comes the sound we want to make!

Good vocal health starts with good overall health. The voice requires the integration of many other parts of our being. Consequently, we should consider a generally healthy lifestyle, which will in turn take care of our voice.

Do:
1. Drink plenty of water
2. Get a good night's sleep
3. Warm up your voice before rigorous singing
4. Practice breath control exercises regularly
5. Do lip trill exercises
6. Exercise regularly and eat properly
7. Maintain a positive spiritual outlook
8. Minimize the use of antihistamine medicines

Don't:
1. Smoke
2 Drink alcohol
3. Speak or sing in dusty environments
4. Shout or engage in prolonged strenuous vocal use
5. Cough excessively

Singing during throat illness is unwise because many illnesses result in inflammation of the vocal folds. Medication intended to treat common illnesses often contains alcohol, which affects the hydration of the vocal folds. Dryness is bad news for the voice. If your day job requires continuous or strenuous use of your voice and then you have to attend a performance or long rehearsal at the end of the day, it is likely that the vocal folds will become swollen. You know your vocal folds are swollen if you find that you can sing a lower note easily and it is difficult to sustain higher notes. This kind of routine, if it becomes a regular tendency, can cause the development of polyps, nodules, or other types of defects on the vocal folds.

Warming up before strenuous vocal use and cooling down afterward will help to minimize damaging effects on the vocal cords. A simple warm-up is to do lip trills or just hum, gliding up and down a pentatonic scale. Humming and doing lip trills after a performance or extended speaking is also good for cooling down and restoring the voice.

VOCAL WARM-UP EXERCISES

"The achievements of an organization are the results of the combined efforts of each individual."

Vince Lombardini

Do not expect that every singer in a choral ensemble will sound like Kathleen Battle, Luciano Pavarotti, or Paul Robeson. In fact, it is better that they don't! It is always a marvel to hear how seemingly ordinary voices can come together to create the beautiful and powerful sound of a choir. Anyone who has heard the Christ Church Cathedral Choir from Oxford, England, The Sixteen, or the Mormon Tabernacle Choir can attest to the sheer beauty and power of the human voice. Individuals will fit into the choir well, once they can comprehend the terms and techniques of the art, and are willing to work with the training regime.

Loud singing is not good for a proper choral tone. First of all, a person who is singing loudly is not able to listen very well. One of the marks of a good singer is having the ability to listen. This applies whether you are a veteran of the art, or a beginner. In fact, significant time must be allocated to ear training exercises.

Let us now look at some group techniques for building the choral tone.

1. Stand with a buoyant posture.

2. Inhale and say "hung" (emphasize the "ng") with an open mouth. While keeping your mouth open, gently change to a sung tone at the pitch level "a," using the vowel sound "ah." That is "hunnng-aaah."

3. Repeat the procedure, substituting the "a" with a "b," and then a "c."

In making the "hung-ah," you should ensure that the soft palate lifts and almost touches the back wall of your throat, and that your jaw is relaxed. In this exercise, the pharynx will be relaxed, the larynx will be relaxed and neutral, the jaw will be low, and the tone will have a free sounding resonance. Strive to keep this basic position as your home position for further exercises. Encourage the singers to feel the sound resonating freely in their mouth space.

4. Practice the wolf howl. Get a nice high howl ("ahwoo") just as the real wolf would. Bring the head tone down to a comfortable pitch, say, a G. Try also to bring the wolf howl tone up from the lower notes. The objective is to find and encourage the singers' head tone. Head tone provides the musical "hum" which creates that choral buzz. With the tone locked in, sing on a pentatonic scale descending then ascending to the sound "loo."

5. Sing chord (F major), or a single note (F), using the "moo" sound, starting at volume level *piano*, and slowly crescendo to *forte*. Next, decrescendo to *piano* (see figure 3). Repeat; this time, start at *pianissimo* and crescendo to *fortissimo*. Finally, decrescendo to *pianissimo*.

6. Sing the word "mum" in a pentatonic scale: "mum, mum, mum, mum, mum," up, and then down. If you start on a chest register pitch, such as G3 below middle C, this exercise will facilitate a

smooth transition from chest to head register as you go up past E4 or F4, above middle C. Encourage the singers to feel the "hum" in their voice, and relax their throat and jaw while doing this exercise.

7. Sing slowly on a three or four note chord, "me, may, mah, moh, moo." Go up in single tone intervals. Ensure that a smooth *legato*, proper posture, vowel placement, and breath support are being observed (see below).

8. Sing "nee" on a *glissando*, or slur, from A3 to A4 and back. Repeat a tone higher and so on up to E4.

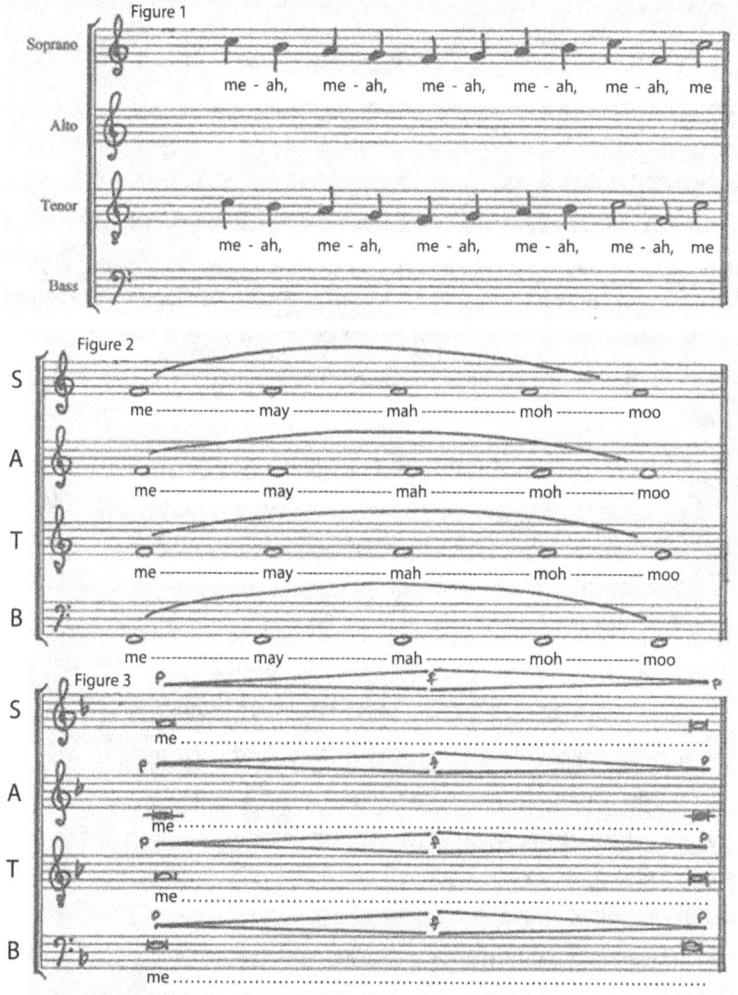

The choir director needs to keenly listen to and guide the singers through these exercises, paying special attention to their posture and breath management. The director must ensure that the "hung" pharyngeal position is being used and that the singers are making a good "hum" in their tone as well. It is good for the director personally to practice these techniques to get a good feel for the sound. If you cup your hands over your ears, you can hear the "hum" in a more intense way.

I recommend the following exercises to help improve breath control:

1. Stand with arms outstretched horizontally to form a cross, palms up.

2. Inhale and simultaneously raise your hands from this position to a position above your head. Count slowly to five as you do so.

3. Hold your breath while slowly lowering your hands to the count of five. You will notice that your chest and posture are dynamically placed as if ready for action. I refer to this as a "buoyant" posture. Maintain this position for a count of five.

4. Exhale in a relaxed manner, but maintain your buoyant posture.

In a buoyant posture, the rib cage is lifted up (imagine an open umbrella) and you must try to keep it that way throughout the singing—even when you have exhausted your breath. It will take practice to do this comfortably.

Here is another exercise:

1. Sit upright, shoulders relaxed, feet apart.

2. Place your hands comfortably on your knees.

3. Inhale deeply through the mouth as if sucking air in through a very small straw. Hold the air and count to five.

4. Exhale as if blowing through the same small straw. Blow the air out on the same count of five until there is no more to blow. At this point your abdomen should be pulled in.

5. Hold this position for another count of five, then inhale and relax.

Notice the deep, low inhalation reaction of the diaphragm when the hold is released. Note also, the outward movement of the abdomen. These exercises will significantly improve your ability to control the air flow because they strengthen the diaphragm. The breath literally "falls" into the lungs.

An alternative exercise which is good for group settings is to have the choir sit forward on their chairs, leaning slightly forward from the hip. Exhale slowly and completely with a hissing sound and hold for a few counts, then release and allow the air to flow rapidly back into the lungs. As before, this will enable a full, low breath.

Here is one vocal exercise you can use to tone your vocal muscles:

1. Stand with a buoyant posture

2. Open your mouth as if to sing "ah" but instead bring your lips to an "oo" position, simulating the yawning throat. Make certain to keep your tongue relaxed. This will open your throat.

3. Bring your chin slightly in toward your chest. Now try to sing a simple tune to the "oo" vowel sound. You will feel a sense of breadth in your sound. The extent of the effect will depend on your natural physical attributes. With practice, this technique will improve the tone of your voice.

4. Gently grasp your throat with your thumb and first finger, just at the position where your larynx can be felt. Say a strong "ee" then "oo." If you do it right, you will feel the definite raising and lowering of your larynx when you say "oo." This is the lowered larynx position.

5. Say the word "hung" with a lowered jaw and an emphasis on the "ng." You will notice that the soft palate feels as if it is trying to touch the upper rear wall of your throat. Repeat the word and this time make the "ng" deep in the back and intense enough to really allow the soft palate to touch the throat wall. Now choose a comfortable pitch and sing "hunnng—ah" The feeling is that the soft palate has risen and there is greater space in the pharyngeal area. The sound is free and resonant. Exercising the soft palate in this way strengthens its response and greatly improves the tone.

Two more exercises:

1. Stand with a buoyant posture, and pant like a dog. At first, make the pants rapid, as if the dog is very hot or has been running. Then gradually (but not too slowly) slow down the rate of panting until it becomes a long deep inhale and exhale. You will feel the action of your diaphragm in a dramatic way. A word of caution: This exercise can lead to hyperventilation and dizziness, so be careful not to overdo it.

2. Hold a square piece of light tissue paper up to your mouth and blow on it steadily to deflect it away from you. Keep blowing to deflect the paper as long as you can manage. Relax and repeat.

These exercises can be done in groups of five repetitions at a time, as part of a warm-up routine. Breath exercises are really designed to improve the muscular strength and tone of the breathing-related muscles, thereby improving the capacity and power of the singing voice. Regular practice will pay off.

The essential aspect of breath management is to have good control over the rate of inhalation, capacity, and the rate of exhalation. In particular, the rate of exhalation determines how the singer manipulates the musical tone. Depending on the type of music, you should try to sing smoothly, and avoid gasping for air in the middle of a phrase.

Some choir directors strive for a crisp, bright tone. A bright tone carries clear diction and resonates well in poor acoustics. However, it is more challenging to produce safely. The key to a bright tone is to focus the tone in the walls of the pharynx rather than in the mask. The tone will still have some head resonance, but only when high notes are involved. In order to develop a bright choral tone, the choir has to practice exercises which encourage forward-placed vowels in the pharynx and the mouth rather than in the mask, such as the "a" in "May" and the "e" in "see." Since many singers have problems finding and using their head voice, I would not recommend venturing into this bright singing tone until your choir is proficient in the use of their head voice.

I suggest using rounds to teach tone, pitch, harmony, and concentration to younger choirs, as they are a lot of fun. Singing in a round is a great way to help the choir sharpen their concentration. Rounds are simple, short tunes which are sung by the group, broken into sub-groups. The first group starts the tune and then a bar or two afterward, the next group starts. A typical round is "Row, row, row your boat." Rounds can be fun to sing, and so even reluctant singers will be encouraged to participate. Singing is about doing. All members of the group must be involved in the exercises. These songs may also be used as warm-ups or to energize the children for more serious work.

Here are some suggested songs to sing in a round:

1. "London Burning" is a simple, basic tune which provides an octave of vocal range, a simple, but effective introduction to harmony, and a mild challenge to the kids' concentration ability. You simply split the group into two parts. One set starts with the first words, "London burning, London burning," then, the second set commences with the same thing, "London burning, London burning." Encourage the kids to have fun with the music, but discourage shouting. "Three Blind Mice" may be used in the same way.

2. "This Old Man" is a great tune for kids, but works even better when teamed up with another great tune: "There Was an Old Man Named Michael Finnegan." Both are sung to the same tune and the simultaneous combination works well to achieve many choral and vocal benefits.

3. "Row, Row, Row Your Boat." This is everybody's first suggestion when the idea of a round comes up. Like the others above, it is simple and effective. There is the added advantage with this one that you can almost give each individual singer their own line.

Summary

*"A person who never made a mistake,
never tried anything new."*
Albert Einstein

How to make your choir great:
1. Audition with purpose. Set your standards.
2. Choose repertoire appropriate for the type of choir and the ability of the singers.
3. Plan rehearsals properly. Anticipate problems.
4. Develop a culture of punctuality. Set the example.
5. Be a 'P' person.
6. Learn about your voice and impart that knowledge to the choir.
7. Teach your choir to adopt proper posture.
8. Teach your choir to breath properly.
9. Pay attention to how vowels are produced.
10. Engage a management team to help you

Glossary of Terms

alveoli. Minute air sacs in the lungs where oxygen is exchanged. Air is stored and used to power the voice.

andante. At a moderate tempo.

appoggio. Italian term for the art of supporting tone through diaphragmatic action and proper posture.

articulation. The process of forming vowels and consonants; involves movement of the tongue and jaw.

aural. Having to do with hearing.

buccal. Mouth-based; referring primarily to the space above the tongue.

bel canto. "Beautiful singing"—an Italian-derived style of tone production, used primarily by choirs and classically trained singers.

belting. Using the speech voice to sing high notes in a forced manner. Mostly used in musical theatre, pop music, and gospel music.

chest voice. Vocal tones characterized by firm vibrations felt in the chest and throat; normal speech voice range.

serratus. Muscle at the upper side of the thorax which can assist in respiration.

crescendo. Gradually getting louder.

diaphragm. Dome-shaped thoracic muscle responsible for inhalation; separates the thorax from the abdomen.

dipthong. Two adjacent vowel sounds with the same syllable.

enunciation. Producing words in a clear manner according to custom. The International Phonetic Alphabet guides singers on correct pronunciation of words in various languages.

epigastrum. Uppermost abdominal muscles, just below the sternum.

epiglottis. Flap of cartilage at the base of the tongue guarding the entrance to the trachea; also used in the production of some vocal sounds.

esophagus. Tube which transports food to the stomach from the mouth.

falsetto. A tone produced in post-puberty males in which the vocal folds touch only at the outer edges; the basis for the countertenor voice.

forte. Loud, strong.

fortissimo. Very loud.

fugue. A complex and highly regimented contrapuntual musical form.

glissando. Singing a scale without making a distinction between individual notes; a "slurring" sound.

head voice. Vocal tone which is characterized by feelings of vibration in the head and face; the characteristic tone of sopranos, trebles, and high tenors.

ichtus. The directional changing point of a conductor's baton signaling a beat; therefore, a three-beat pattern has three points.

larynx. The organ of vocal sound production.

legato. Smoothly connected phrasing.

mask. The face area encompassing the nose, cheeks, and temples; carries a "humming" sensation when tone is produced in a certain way.

messa di voce. Vocal exercise in which the tone crescendos and decrescendos.

mezzo forte. Moderately loud.

mezzo piano. Moderately soft.

modal voice. Normal everyday speech voice.

nasal. Having to do with the nasal cavities.

oral. Having to do with the mouth space.

passagio. Perceived area of tone transition from chest register to head register.

pharynx. The internal area of the upper and lower throat space.

phonation. Process of producing vocal tone; involves complex muscle activity.

piano. Soft.

pianissimo. Very soft.

register. A range of vocal tones produced with a recognizable sound quality.

resonation. Process of enhancing a basic tone with desirable sound qualities.

resonance. Vocal amplification through the encouragement of certain vibration frequencies in the voice, utilizing the throat, chest, and nasal passages.

respiration. The process of taking air into the body.

ritenuto. Hold back, slower.

staccato. Singing very short notes in a rapid sequence, making each note distinguished with a soft "h."

sinus. Sponge-like cavities in the facial bones which resonate with certain tones.

treble. The high tone of a young male singer with an unchanged voice in the soprano range.

tessitura. The vocal range which provides the most efficient tone production.

trachea. Tube which facilitates air passage into and out of the lungs.

thorax. Chest.

tone. A vocal sound.

uvela. The soft palate. The section of the roof of the mouth which seems to hang down at the back of the throat when you view it in a mirror.

vocal. Having to do with the voice and tone production.

About the Author

The wonderful Kingston College Chapel Choir in Kingston, Jamaica, inspired me to take up the challenge of choir directing twenty-seven years ago. I joined the Chapel Choir as a treble in 1976 and became its director in 1985. Exposure, formal voice training, choral directing, and experience with individuals of all ages and abilities have allowed me to develop many techniques  and procedures to bring out the best in any group of singers. I have been privileged to conduct works such as Benjamin Britten's "*Rejoice in the Lamb*," G. F. Handel's "Dixit Dominus," "Chandos Anthems," and *Zadok the Priest*, Joseph Haydn's "Te Deum," Gregorio Allegri's *Miserere mei Deus*, Giovanni Palestrina's *Missa Papae Marcelli*, among others. I have done numerous television appearances, tours, and live recordings with the Chapel Choir. My work has involved annual choir workshops with both traditional and charismatic church choirs, as well as amateur singers and singing groups. I also teach music and singing to children from kindergarten to high school, and hold private voice classes.

Founded in 1947, the Kingston College Chapel Choir is a men and boys high school choir which has had a long tradition of choral excellence, rivaling the best anywhere in the world. The choir has achieved and maintained this reputation despite never having had the type of resources which one would associate with a choir which performs at that level, as well as drawing its membership from diverse socioeconomic backgrounds, musical cultures, and religious denominations. This is a choir of ordinary boys and young men, whose musical expertise is developed solely within the choir, but which nevertheless has resulted in an extraordinary choir. Noted past directors include Rev. Dr. Barry Davies, organist; Gordon Appleton, regional director of the RSCM; Donald Morris, director of the Newark Boy's Chorus and Choir School. It is this musical background which has nurtured my own development and indeed that of many other musicians.